WHEN CHRISTIANS GET IT WRONG

ADAM HAMILTON

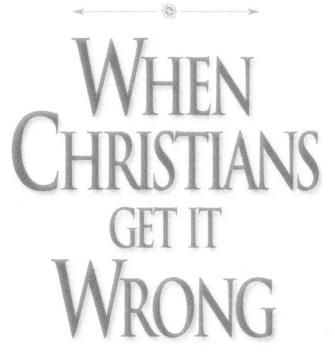

WHEN CHRISTIANS GET IT WRONG

Updated & Revised

Abingdon Press / Nashville

WHEN CHRISTIANS GET IT WRONG

Copyright © 2010, 2013 by Abingdon Press

All rights reserved.

Library of Congress Cataloging-in-Publication Data

Hamilton, Adam, 1964–
   When Christians get it wrong / Adam Hamilton.
      p.   cm.
   ISBN 978-1-4267-7523-9 (book- pbk./trade pbk. : alk. paper) 1.
Apologetics.   2. Christian life.   I. Title.
   BT1103.H35   2010
   239'.7—dc22

                                                              2010019358

Scripture quotations unless noted otherwise are taken from the New Revised Standard Version of the Bible, copyright 1989 by the Division of Christian Education of the National Council of the Churches of Christ in the United States of America. Used by permission. All rights reserved.

Scripture quotations marked NIV are taken from the Holy Bible, NEW INTERNATIONAL VERSION®. Copyright © 1973, 1978, 1984 by the International Bible Society. All rights reserved throughout the world. Used by permission of the International Bible Society.

13 14 15 16 17 18 19 20 21 22—10 9 8 7 6 5 4 3 2 1

A

To John

CONTENTS

Introduction   1

1. When Christians Are UnChristian   5

2. Christians, Science, and Politics   21

3. When Speaking of Other Religions   37

4. When Bad Things Happen   57

5. In Dealing with Homosexuality   79

6. When Christians Get It Right   97

The Conversation Continues:
God and Public Schools   109

Postscript   113

INTRODUCTION

This book was born out of a conversation with a young man who had some pretty strong negative perceptions of the Christian faith. As I listened to him, I realized that he was rejecting a God that I, too, had rejected years earlier. He described many of the same frustrations I had as a pastor with how Christians sometimes act and with the beliefs about God that many Christians hold.

A few years ago, David Kinnaman and Gabe Lyon published the results of their research with young adults who are disengaged from the church—men and women like John—and their findings closely mirrored John's concerns. Kinnaman and Lyon's book, *unChristian*, focused largely on the attitudes and behaviors exhibited by some Christians that young adults found off-putting. They found

1

that 91 percent of young adults who are not involved in church described Christians as anti-homosexual, 87 percent of them described Christians as judgmental, and 85 percent of them described Christians as hypocritical.[1]

Kinnaman and Lyon and a host of others have focused on the attitudes and actions of Christians that have turned young adults away from the Christian faith. But my conversation with John, and with a number of other young adults, indicates that it is not only the attitudes and actions of Christians that are off-putting but also the theological convictions that often give rise to these actions. John and other young adults I have spoken with take issue with Christian *doctrine* (or belief) as it has been expressed to them by many Christians—doctrines related to suffering, science and faith, the Bible, salvation, and the final judgment, particularly as it relates to non-Christians.

In this book I seek to address both the attitudes and actions of Christians who get it wrong *and* the beliefs that are most often cited as problematic by non-Christians. At the end of each chapter, I also offer suggestions on what it looks like when Christians get it right.

This book is intended for two audiences: The first is young adults who are turning away from Christianity in larger numbers than previous generations did at the same age and stage in life. I hope the book will be read by college students and young adults who don't go to church, who have been frustrated and turned off by what they have heard from and experienced with Christians. The second audience is Christians; I invite them to examine their attitudes, actions, and beliefs. I offer a different way of understanding some very serious theological issues—related to the nature of God, Scripture, science and faith, the religions of the world, and homosexuality—from what is often articulated by the loudest Christian voices in the current culture.

I am grateful for the team at Abingdon Press. They have been patient, encouraging, and tremendously helpful in bringing this book to publication. I am honored to be in partnership and ministry with them. Thank you!

I hope and pray that this book will help some young adults find faith once more and become followers of Jesus Christ. It is also my hope that the book might chart a path for Christians in how we can "get it right." Churches that "get it wrong" may lose an entire generation of young adults, the future of the church. Those that get it right have a "future with hope" (Jeremiah 29:11).

Adam Hamilton

1. See David Kinnaman and Gabe Lyon, *unChristian* (Grand Rapids, Mich.: Baker Books, 2007), or visit www.unchristian.com.

CHAPTER ONE

WHEN CHRISTIANS ARE UNCHRISTIAN

John was twenty-four years old and had just returned from six years as an Army Airborne Ranger deployed first in Afghanistan and then in Iraq. It was John's dad, Tom, who suggested we meet. I am Tom's pastor. Tom told me that John had very strong negative feelings about the Christian faith. He felt that both John and I would benefit from a conversation together. We met in my office, and in our ninety-minute conversation John was thoughtful, articulate, and respectful, but at times almost angry as he described for me the reasons he had rejected Christianity. His subtle undertone of anger was not directed toward me, but at the views, attitudes, and actions of Christians he had known—views that seemed out of sync with the God of love that Christianity preached. John was describing for me the ways in which he believed Christians get it wrong.

John's feelings about Christians were not new to me. I had heard them many times before, though seldom as thoughtfully or comprehensively presented as John presented them. I had felt some of these same things myself in dealing with some of my fellow Christians. Several years after meeting John, our church set up a Web site to invite young adults (those under thirty-five) to tell us where they believe Christians get it wrong. About that same time we began sitting down to talk with people who had opted out of church. There were so many common responses between the two groups. Generally we found that young people rejected Christianity because of the beliefs, attitudes, and actions of Christians they knew.

Their criticism of Christianity usually included one or more of five key themes: (1) the unChristian ways some Christians act, (2) the anti-intellectual, antiscience stance of some Christians, (3) Christianity's views of other world religions, (4) questions related to the role of God in human suffering, and (5) the way Christians view homosexuality. Each of these themes will be considered in a chapter in this book.

My hope in writing this book is to speak for young adults who have been turned off, frustrated, or even hurt by Christians and to suggest what Christianity might look like when Christians get it right. Let's begin with the unChristian ways some Christians act.

When Christians
Are UnChristian

In their 2007 book, *unChristian* (Baker Books), David Kinnaman and Gabe Lyons outlined the research of the Barna Group with hundreds of young adults who, like John in our opening story, were outside the Christian faith. They found that more young adults today are turning away from Christianity than in years past. Their research did not explore the theological issues that have turned people away from the Christian faith; instead they focused on understanding the perceptions non-Christian young adults have of Christians. Among their findings:

- 91% of those adults surveyed who were outside the Christian faith felt Christians were "anti-homosexual."
- 87% felt Christians were judgmental.
- 85% felt Christians were hypocritical.
- 75% felt Christians were too political.
- 70% thought Christians were insensitive.[1]

My conversations with young adults substantiate these findings. If these words accurately describe how young adults have experienced Christians, then is it any surprise that they are turning away from the Christian faith in droves?

When I ask non-Christians what they think Jesus stood for, most say, "Love." And they are correct; this is one of the defining elements of Jesus' teaching. He told his followers that God's will for humanity could be summarized with two commands: love God and love your neighbor. He went on to say that our neighbor is anyone who needs our help. The love we are to show is not a feeling but a way of acting—a love of kindness and compassion and a desire to bless and seek good for others. Jesus told his disciples they were to love not only their neighbors and friends but their enemies as well. He told them that the world would know that they are his disciples by their love. Non-Christians know that Jesus stood for love. Which is why, when those who claim to follow Jesus act in unloving ways, it feels particularly unpleasant.

This disparity between the love Christians are meant to display and what young adults often experience is most pronounced when Christians speak with judgment or in disparaging ways toward others.

One young man described an experience when he was invited to attend a special youth group event at a big church in his town. He noted that the kids at school rarely spoke to him until it was "bring a friend day" at youth group. They invited him to join their group at the local water park. Here's his description of how the day went:

It didn't start off badly; the rides at the park were fun, and I even enjoyed hanging out with some of them. But during the long ride back to the church, they started talking about people. They discussed who was having sex, who was smoking weed, who was gay. The more they talked the worse things they said. Many of the people they were talking about were my friends, and they knew it! To make things worse, some of the ones talking loudest were doing the very things they were gossiping about. Finally, they got on to the subject of who was going to hell. It seems that if you didn't go to their brand of church, you didn't stand a chance of getting into heaven. That, of course, meant me, and it didn't seem to matter to them at all that I was sitting right there, soaking all this up.

The judgmental, hypocritical, and unloving spirit these Christians displayed left this young man determined not to go back to church.

Another young woman echoed these same sentiments when she said:

I'm thinking of the Christians in my school that I see every day. They judge everyone constantly. It's annoying, and a lot of people don't really like it or like them because of it. I have a really good friend who claims to be a really hard-core Christian but he smokes weed all the time and drinks and does all these things and lies, and he's just not a Christian at all.

These were both teens who turned away from the Christian faith because of the actions of Christians they knew. But this phenomenon is not unique to young adults. No doubt you can think of examples of Christians you have known who were judgmental, hypocritical, and unloving.

Some of the most insensitive, critical, judgmental, and mean-spirited people I've known were persons who claimed to be committed Christians.

I was officiating at the graveside funeral for a young man who had taken his own life. The parents were still in shock and experiencing intense grief. In the eulogy and message I sought to help them and all who had gathered to make sense of this terrible tragedy while finding comfort and hope in God. As a part of the service we remembered the unique and special qualities of their son. Following the service, a husband and wife—sister and brother-in-law of one of the boy's parents—came to me and asked, "Why didn't you tell them that their son is in hell today?" I was taken aback and asked, "How do you know the boy is in hell today? Do you know what was in the boy's heart? Are you so certain you know the mind of God?" They looked at me and walked away. What kind of people are so certain of another's eternal fate that they can stand before grieving parents and callously tell them their son is in hell?

I could fill this book with stories like these from my own personal experience of Christians, including a few pastors I know, who are free with their condemnation of everyone who doesn't conform to their very narrow view of the world, of the Bible, and of truth.

Jesus and the Pharisees

Of course Jesus confronted the same kinds of things in his day. If you read the Gospels carefully, Jesus never got angry with prostitutes, adulterers, or ordinary "sinners." Nor did his actions turn such people away. In fact, Jesus drew "sinners" to himself by the thousands. He made such people feel at ease. The only people Jesus had words of judgment for in the Gospels were the religious folks. What angered him the most about these people, particularly the religious leaders, was their judgmentalism, their hypocrisy, and their failure to love. They believed God was primarily interested in people following the rules. Jesus taught that God's primary rule was love, and that God's interest wasn't in condemning "sinners" but in drawing them to God.

11

Though Jesus was opposed by various people in the Gospels, his primary opposition was from a group of religious people called Pharisees (the word likely comes from a Hebrew word that means "set apart" or "separated"). They believed that holiness and a life pleasing to God came from separating yourself from sin and in obeying the commands of God. This all makes sense but, like many modern-day Christians, they had missed the point. They failed to see that God's primary concern is not rules, but people. They should have been celebrating the fact that thousands of people who had turned away from organized religion were drawn to hear Jesus teach about the kingdom of God. Instead they were repulsed by Jesus' willingness to associate with people "like that." In response, Jesus spoke some pretty harsh words to the Pharisees and the other religious leaders of his time. The word he used most frequently to describe them in the Gospels is the Greek word *hupokrisis* from which we have the word *hypocrisy*. The Greek word was used to refer to an actor in a play—a pretender.

The truth is, we are all in danger of being "pretenders" when it comes to our highest values and aspirations. This is particularly true for religious people, which is why Jesus often warned his disciples about hypocrisy, warnings that covered four different expressions of hypocrisy: wrong motives, judging others, "majoring in the minors," and being two-faced. Let's briefly consider what Jesus warned against in each of these areas.

1. Wrong Motives

Once when Jesus was talking to his followers, he warned them about the dangers of praying, fasting, and helping out the poor. Why would he do that? Aren't all of those good things? Yes they are, unless you do them for the wrong reasons. If you pray and fast out of a genuine desire to get closer to God, you do well. The same is true if you give money to the poor because you sincerely wish to lessen their burdens.

But that's not why everyone does these things. Jesus talked about people who would pray on street corners, blow a loud trumpet when they were about to give to a needy person, and make sure everyone who saw them knew they were fasting. Why? So that other people (people like them) would know how "religious" they were, and praise them for it. They were using God and their religion to further their careers, or their stature in the community, or to meet their needs for affirmation from others (see Matthew 6:1-8, 16-18).

2. Pointing out the Sin of Others Without Seeing Our Own

One of the strangest things Jesus ever said had to do with lumber (makes sense coming from a carpenter, doesn't it?). He asked some religious leaders how they could criticize people who had a speck of sawdust in their eye, while the leaders didn't notice the two-by-four lodged in their own eyes (Matthew 7:1-5). What did he mean? He was referring to religious people who readily point out the sins of others while failing to see their own shortcomings. They demonstrate a kind of superiority and spiritual or moral pride, but they fail to see that their pride is actually a more sinister and deadly sin than the sins of those they are denouncing. Jesus then called his hearers to remove the "log" from their own eye before seeking to remove the speck from another's eye. In essence he was saying, "Stop pointing out the sins of others; you've got enough issues of your own!"

3. Majoring in Minors

If you grew up where and when Jesus did, you were encouraged to tithe, that is, contribute a tenth of your income to support the Temple and other religious causes. Some of Jesus' religious contemporaries had this figured out in great detail. You know those herbs you grow on your windowsill, the little ones? Well these folks would even take the clippings from those plants, separate out a tenth of them, and contribute even that. No one was going to accuse them of not living up to their obligations!

Jesus did, however. Calling them "blind guides," he reminded them that while tithing is good, they were missing the more important matters like living a life of justice and mercy toward their neighbors (Matthew 23:23-24).

I've known people who called themselves Christians, who were convinced that they alone were right, and who were willing to fight over the tiniest, least consequential of things. We Christians argue over forms of baptism, our interpretation of minor points of Scripture, even the forms of music we play in church. Christians have fought entire wars over our sectarian differences, all the while forgetting that Jesus said that the defining characteristic of a Christian's life is meant to be love.

4. Being Two-faced

You probably know people who appear to be one thing when you first meet them, but upon getting to know them better you find they are something else entirely. Jesus knew people like this, too. He once suggested that such people are like a person who washes the outside of a dirty cup but fails to wash the inside, so the drink that remains inside the cup spoils—I picture the glasses of milk or soda I used to find in my teenage daughter's room that had been sitting there for weeks—curdled, moldy, and with the rankest of smells (Luke 11:39)!

Jesus was speaking of a superficial faith, which is seen in the outward appearance of religious behavior but has not sunk down into the heart. Like those who focus on the minutiae, these people have missed the bigger point of faith. Their religion is skin deep and hasn't addressed the really serious issues in their hearts or the truly important issues of society. Not all Pharisees were hypocrites, but many seemed to miss the point in this way.

This description also applies to too many Christians I know. They understand how to do religious things but fail to let their religion change their values, their hearts, and ultimately their daily lives. Their religion is window dressing.

In a prophetic warning to his disciples, Jesus says in Luke 12:1, "Beware of the yeast of the Pharisees, that is, their hypocrisy." Why did Jesus warn the disciples against becoming hypocrites? Because he knew that his own followers would not be immune to this common temptation for religious people.

We Are All Recovering Pharisees

Today's Pharisees are religious people who struggle with wrong motives, with being critical and judgmental of others, with missing the point, and with being two-faced. I've got to confess, unfortunately, that I am a recovering Pharisee—one who often falls off the wagon. Everyone I know, religious people and atheists alike, struggles with these four tendencies.

It is so easy to do the right things for all the wrong reasons. It is so easy to point out the sins of others while ignoring our own. Most of us are experts at "majoring in the minors" while failing to do the really important things God demands of us. And which of us has never put on a face and pretended to be something we're not? It is only in recognizing our tendency to be Pharisees that we have any hope of remaining in recovery.

My experience with non-religious people is that they do not expect Christians to be perfect. In fact, one young adult said, "I don't mind that you Christians don't live up to your ideals. I don't live up to all of my ideals either. In the end, I guess we're all hypocrites. It's just that I and my friends recognize that we're hypocrites. It seems that many Christians haven't figured this out yet." Again, the hypocrisy of Christians is most troubling to new Christians when we point out the sins of others.

Getting It Right

Every Christian gets it wrong sometimes. The critique from John in our opening story and from the countless others who share with him a frustration with Christian hypocrisy is an important wake-up call—a warning to Christians who are becoming the very Pharisees Jesus preached against.

When Christians are judgmental, hypocritical, insensitive, and mean-spirited, they are acting in ways that are unChristian. When the apostle Paul described what Christians should strive to be like, he used these words: love, joy, peace, patience, kindness, gentleness, generosity, faithfulness, and self-control (Galatians 5:22-23). UnChristian Christians stand out because even non-Christians know that these people are living in a way that is inconsistent with Jesus' teaching. Jesus commanded his followers not to judge. He warned them against hypocrisy. Again and again he called them to love all, both their neighbors and those with whom they did not see eye to eye.

For all the Christians who get it wrong, I believe there are many who get it right. They are not as vocal as their pharisaic counterparts. And they are not perfect. But there really are countless Christians who daily seek to live authentic lives of faith. They go out of their way to care for others. They are compassionate. They live and give sacrificially to others. They volunteer their time to serve the poor, or visit the sick, or take the time to encourage the discouraged. They work for justice. They genuinely love people.

When I asked John if he knew any Christians like this he spoke about Margie, a friend he described as "the real thing." She cared about John. She did not judge him. She is a thoughtful, intelligent, and committed Christian who has shown love to John whether he became a Christian or not.

When I think of Christians who get it right, I think of Kathy. She cuts hair in a salon in the basement of her home, and I sit in her barber chair once a month. I go as much to be inspired as I do to have my hair cut. This woman has a heart of compassion that won't quit. Every month she shares a story of some project she hopes our church will get behind. Since she has scissors in her hands, I'm all ears! She has started and organized a variety of ministries to care for the homeless in our city. Perhaps my favorite is her work in cutting the hair of the homeless. I had never thought about where the homeless go for a haircut. But Kathy did. She had our church install chairs and sinks at several of the city's missions. Then she organized a team of barbers and stylists to go to these different missions throughout the month to offer free haircuts. She said:

> Adam, most of these men haven't had another human being touch them in years. But when they sit in my chair, they are inviting me to touch them. I can feel them tense up at first, and then they relax. My prayer is that somehow, as

I am touching them, cutting and styling their hair, they feel God's love for them through me. I don't care what they've done in the past, or whether they've bathed, or how they ended up homeless. I know their lives matter to God and that they are valuable to him.... When I am finished, I can see a visible change in these men and women. They look at themselves in the mirror as they rise from my chair and I sense that they remember that they are somebody—that their lives have value—all because of a haircut.

I think that's what it looks like when Christians get it right.

When Christians get it right they love and give, they work for justice and demonstrate kindness. When Christians get it right they, like Jesus, befriend those who are outside the church rather than condemning them. And when Christians get it right, people are drawn to, rather than repelled by, their faith.

1. *unChristian*, 28.

CHAPTER TWO

CHRISTIANS, SCIENCE, AND POLITICS

Science, Faith, and Fear

As John and I talked, he told me that it was not just the hypocrisy of Christians that troubled him. He was also turned off by the way many Christians approached modern science. John noted:

> The whole question of creationism versus evolution and scientific theory is always something that bothered me. You know that people will tell you God created all of this ten thousand years ago in the blink of an eye; there you go. But when you honestly look at science and evolution—the miraculous complexity of it all and the beauty of how the system works—I've actually asked people, "Don't you see anything divine in that?" "Oh no, no, no." And people will pass off the creation story in the blink of an eye because it's accepted and it's in the Bible. Well, you know

> what, there are a lot of things in the Bible that were writ-
> ten two thousand years ago; and how can we honestly
> interpret what those men were saying in modern termi-
> nology? When people tell me creationism is in the Bible,
> that is just a statement to me of how exceedingly ignorant
> someone is. I don't like to blatantly label people as idiots,
> but I think of them as less intellectually active.

This is the perception that many thinking people have of Christians—that they are "less intellectually active."

To hear some Christians talk, you would think we are starring in our own version of the movie *Groundhog Day*, waking up morning after morning to find that it's June 22, 1633. That's when a tribunal of the church pronounced Galileo a heretic for promoting the shocking notion that the earth moves around the sun, not the other way around. They made Galileo take back what he had said (which he seems to have done with his fingers crossed behind his back), and then placed him under house arrest to prevent him from spreading any more dangerous ideas.

Today, of course, it is common and accepted knowledge that the sun sits at the center of our solar system, and that there are likely countless other solar systems with planets also circling their own stars among all the galaxies flung through-out the universe. In other words, what was a dangerous and heretical idea on June 22, 1633, is now something most people (including most Christians) take for granted. I wonder how many of the issues over which Christians battle with science today will take a similar path.

If Christian attitudes toward science bother you, then you are not alone. Surveys of young adults show that many bright, thinking people find themselves increasingly alienated by the belief, expressed by some Christians, that much of what we know from modern science is incompatible with Christian teaching. This is not a new development, of course. Galileo's trial was only the start of an accelerating process in which scientific discoveries have drawn the wrath of Christians who complain that the new ideas undermine their faith. From discoveries in geology about the age of the earth to the much-maligned science of evolution, some Christians have been pushing back at advances in science for centuries.

As I try to understand why so many Christians carry on this battle with science, I keep coming back to one word: *fear*. Simply put, Christians are afraid that science will disprove or debunk what they believe. They secretly worry that the next scientific development will be the one that decisively shows that God doesn't exist, that the gospel is a fraud. They think that the more people know about science, the less they will believe in God. Christians fear science because they think that it either competes with faith or is actively engaged in destroying faith. They think that science leaves no room for God; if you let it get its foot in the door, science will take over the whole house.

But God is not threatened by science. If creation is the handiwork of God, and science helps us see the exquisite and marvelous workings of creation, how can that do anything but magnify God for people of faith?

Several years ago I had the opportunity to visit the Sistine Chapel in Rome. As I stood there looking up at Michelangelo's magnificent frescoes on the chapel ceiling, a docent came up and asked if I'd like to know more about the work. I said, "Please. I know a little, but I'd like to know more!" She told me that Michelangelo labored for four years to complete the work, and that it is considered one of the most important works in the history of art. She described techniques Michelangelo used, some of which he pioneered, in order to leave such a legacy. She even told me that one of the "facts" I had always been taught about the painting was wrong—Michelangelo did not lie on his back to paint; he stood on the scaffolding and cocked his head back (a far more uncomfortable position)! Do you think I was less in awe by virtue of having the docent's explanations? The docent's insights and knowledge led me to an immensely greater appreciation of the Sistine Ceiling and Michelangelo's artistry.

In the same way, scientists act as God's docents, whether they believe in God or not. By helping us understand God's handiwork, they add to the majesty and glory of creation that, as a believer, leaves me with a greater sense of awe about the One who created all things.

I am an amateur astronomer. I have an 8" Meade LX90 Schmidt-Cassegraine telescope at home that I take out to my backyard to tour the galaxy on warm nights. I begin with a glance at Saturn's rings and Jupiter's moons, but then I head off to the Hercules Cluster and then view a variety of nebula, stars, and galaxies. I turn my scope toward the Milky Way's nearest neighbor, the Andromeda Galaxy. Through my scope it is only a small gray smudge. But here's what I find mind-boggling: The light in that smudge took two million years to reach my eye, traveling at the rate of 186,000 miles per second! And this is our nearest neighbor—part of the "local group" of galaxies. And here's how I feel as I stand in the darkness of my backyard: I feel small, and that leads me to realize how truly big God is. Astronomy leads me to say with the psalmist, "The heavens are telling the glory of God" (Psalm 19:1). I stand in the backyard and find myself driven to awe and wonder and praise.

When some Christians add up the ages represented by the genealogies of the Old Testament and then tell us that the earth is less than ten thousand years old, I want to laugh or cry. With John, I find myself wondering why they can't appreciate that the biblical stories of creation were written in the form of Hebrew poetry. They were not written as God's way of giving ancient people a lesson in cosmology or biology or physics. They were written to say that behind all of the magnificent beauty of creation there is One who created—who called for all that is and gave it form and shape and established the laws and patterns that govern it.

In the twentieth century, many Christians opposed evolution. Not all Christians held this opinion, but some of the most vocal Christians did. They felt that evolution (at least at the "macro" level) somehow undermines the glory of God. They believed that God had to have created each species, from scratch, rather than overseeing a process by which simpler life forms became more complex. The most famous of the battles between Christianity and evolution was played out in a courtroom in Dayton, Tennessee, in July 1925. In March of that year the Tennessee legislature had made it illegal to teach any theory that contradicted the creation of humankind as taught in the Bible. Christian attorney William Jennings Bryan won the case, and high school teacher John Scopes was found guilty of breaking the law. The constitutionality of the law was upheld; it was not repealed until 1967. Bryan may have won the case, but in the realm of public opinion, it was Christianity that lost and appeared to be backward in its thinking.

In the latter part of the twentieth century, the battle was on again as fundamentalists challenged textbooks and demanded that creationism be taught alongside evolution.

To many Christians, evolution is simply a way of describing a process that God established for creating the magnificent forms of life we have today. Henry Ford designed the automobile assembly line. He approved the designs of his cars. His name appears on every car. Yet he did not personally build each car. They were his design. His fingerprints were all over the process. Millions of Fords were produced during his watch over the company. No one says that because Ford didn't personally build each car with his own hands he wasn't ultimately responsible for the Ford automobile. If there had been no Henry Ford, there would have been no Ford Automobile Company. Think of creation in this way: God created the processes and the plans for progression of life on our planet. God is still the Creator. Whether each species was individually crafted by God, or the result of a process God designed matters little to me. God remains the Creator either way.

Science and faith are two different ways of understanding our existence. Science helps us understand the physical processes—how the universe works. This is hugely important and, as I've already noted, no threat to genuine faith. Theology and faith, on the other hand, aim to teach us what our existence means. While science asks the questions *what* and *how*, theology seeks to answer the questions *why* and for *what purpose*. Both sets of questions are important.

Can science *by itself* answer questions of ultimate meaning? No. Science isn't equipped or designed to address these questions. A Phillips-head screwdriver is a wonderful tool for tightening and loosening screws. But if you need to paint a wall, that screwdriver is just not the right tool for the job. And that's how it is when you try to use science to answer questions of purpose and meaning. It's not going to help because that is not the job it was designed to do. And when we try to use the Bible to answer scientific questions, it's a bit like trying to use a paintbrush to drive screws into a wall. It is the wrong tool for the job.

This is why Christians get it wrong when they treat the book of Genesis as a science textbook. It stands to reason that if you look in the wrong place for something, you are not going to find it. If you pick up a detective novel expecting to find a recipe for cherry pie, you will be disappointed. The same is true if you go looking for "who done it" in a cookbook. So why do many Christians think they will find a scientific explanation of the origins of the universe in a poetic narrative about God the Creator?

The creation stories in Genesis were not meant to teach us *how* God created, but *that* God created. They are written in deliberately dramatic and vivid language; I hear music when

I read them. They are meant to stir the soul with the image of God calling forth light from darkness then creating the earth, sun, moon, and stars, all the creatures of the land and sea, and finally human beings themselves. The stories teach us that there is a God, that God is good, that creation is a good gift of God, and that human beings are created in God's image (not in our physical appearance, but in our capacity to love, to think, to reason, to make moral decisions, and to act as co-creators with God).

Several years ago, to help our congregation see how science and faith are not enemies but companions in a search for knowledge and truth, I preached a series of sermons titled "Where Science and Religion Meet."[1] We went to area universities, including the University of Kansas and the University of Missouri in Kansas City, and interviewed professors of astrophysics, biology, psychology, and others. We wanted people to see that one does not have to choose between science and faith but that both are valuable partners in understanding our place in the universe. To the surprise of some people, the study of science, far from damaging their faith, actually deepened it.

One young man who joined us for that particular sermon series—watching each sermon online[2]—was an evolutionary biologist and professor at Cornell University named Scott Williamson. Scott's work on recent evolutionary changes in the human genome was chosen as number forty-three of the one hundred most important scientific discoveries of 2007 by *Discover Magazine*. Scott, who considered himself an atheist, was in Kansas City at Christmas and had attended the Christmas Eve service when we announced this sermon series. He was intrigued that a church was willing to approach science and scientists not as enemies, but as colleagues on a quest for truth. He watched each sermon and later wrote to say that, though he had been a lifelong atheist, the sermon series had convinced him that it was possible to be a "scientist and thinking person." He wrote that he had come to believe in the existence of God. He also noted that his wife's love had also played a key role in experiencing the love of God. Scott was diagnosed with a brain tumor shortly after this and died a year later. Before he died, we had opportunities to e-mail and talk by phone and in person as he was deepening his newfound faith and seeking to understand the significance of the Christian gospel as he approached death.

Scott's story points to the importance of both science and faith. Scott was doing very important work at Cornell in the area of biology—making discoveries that answered the *how* and *what* questions. But he began to long for more. He wanted to know why and for what purpose. He wanted to know if there was a God who really did know and love him. He wanted to know if he would continue to live after his physical body succumbed to cancer. These were not questions science could answer. As Scott's physical illness progressed, we talked about the resurrection of Jesus and the hope of the biblical authors that this world is not all that there is to existence. I read the words of the apostle Paul to him from 2 Corinthians 4:16–5:1:

> So we do not lose heart. Even though our outer nature is wasting away, our inner nature is being renewed day by day. For this slight momentary affliction is preparing us for an eternal weight of glory beyond all measure, because we look not at what can be seen but at what cannot be seen; for what can be seen is temporary, but what cannot be seen is eternal. For we know that if the earthly tent we live in is destroyed, we have a building from God, a house not made with hands, eternal in the heavens.

And we talked about trusting God with our lives and trusting in Christ whose death and resurrection can give us life and hope.

Shortly before Scott's death, he had compasses engraved for his young daughters—he loved hiking with them and he wanted to leave them something that would guide them long after he was gone. On the compasses the engraving read, "I will be with you wherever, whenever, forever." He said to his

31

wife, Shannon, shortly before his death, "I will love you forever." His hope of watching his children even after his death and of loving his wife forever came not from the field of science but from his newfound faith.

Christians get it wrong when they see science as a threat to faith, or when they try to make the Bible a scientific textbook. But they get it right when they see science as an important companion in the quest for knowledge and truth.

Postscript: Politics and Religion

Let's consider another area where young people believe Christians get it wrong. I recently received an e-mail from a young woman in response to my request for stories of when Christians get it wrong. She told me that she had not grown up in church, but that in recent months she had become a Christian and joined a church. She also said that she was a Democrat, and that when she became a Christian she thought that her political beliefs on issues like poverty, education, the environment, and health care were a good fit for her Christian convictions on compassion and care of others. But that's not what some of the folks at her church thought. She came away from conversations with them sensing that they believed that her political and social views were inconsistent with her newfound faith. More than one person implied that she couldn't be both a Christian and a Democrat.

This young adult, who has recently joined the faith, was essentially being told that her kind wasn't welcome in the church she had just joined and that her political views might keep her out of heaven. I wondered what kind of church would say such things. Aren't committed and idealistic young folks like her precisely the sort of people churches should be reaching out to? I wrote to ask her what church she belonged to where some Christians said this to her. To my surprise and disappointment she said that she had joined the church I pastor!

I pastor a church in a predominantly "red" state, yet our congregation is divided between Democrats and Republicans. We have leaders and elected officials from both parties, including our state's Democratic Governor and several Republican legislators. I appreciate some elements of both parties and disagree with others. I have voted for persons in both parties. I am convinced that Jesus would not perfectly fit either of them. But I think the way Christians sometimes engage in politics has been damaging, particularly for many young adults. I received the following note from one of our older parishioners when I asked about how Christians get it wrong in politics:

Your question caused a rush of memories of our most recent national political campaign. We have a number of very close friends who are passionate about their politics. They regularly profess their strong Christian commitments, but somehow have a blind spot when it comes to how they react to views and opinions of those with whom they differ. . . .When we get close to that political arena, I have trouble sensing any Christian love or tolerance of any perspective but their own.

But it is deeper than attitude and opinions. Some Christians, in the name of God, say and do things in the realm of politics that are the antithesis of the gospel: slander, gossip, malicious talk, mean-spirited rhetoric, disrespect, and worse. This has been particularly true when it comes to spreading rumors and half-truths using the Internet. I am disappointed at how often Christians I know forward slanderous e-mail to everyone on their e-mail list without taking the time to verify the claims in the message. It doesn't matter whether you are a Democrat or a Republican, you have a moral and spiritual responsibility not to slander or send out inflammatory e-mails about the opposing party or its candidates.

The apostle Paul offers instructions for Christians to conduct themselves in all areas of life. These words are particularly pertinent when it comes to politics:

> Let no evil talk come out of your mouths, but only what
> is useful for building up, as there is need, so that your
> words may give grace to those who hear.... Put away from
> you all bitterness and wrath and anger and wrangling and
> slander, together with all malice, and be kind to one
> another. (Ephesians 4:29-32)

Paul notes that when we act in belligerent ways we "grieve
the Holy Spirit of God." The Greek word for grieve means to
"inflict distress or intense sadness upon." That is what Christians do to God when they speak words that tear others down,
or that slander them. Christians are called to speak words that
"give grace"—that is, undeserved kindness—to all.

Christians should be engaged in the political arena. I
encourage our church members to consider civil service as a
calling. But Christians get it wrong in the area of politics
when they too closely associate their faith with a political
party, or they lay aside Christian ethics and Christ's call to
love even our enemies, and instead they engage in slander and
mean-spirited partisan politics. Christians get it right when
they work for justice, and when grace, truth, and love mark
their political activities.

1. This series of sermons is now available on audio CD or DVD at
http://thewell.cor.org.
2. Our worship services are streamed every weekend and the sermons are
posted for free download as podcasts or can be viewed online. Visit our Web
site at http://www.cor.org.

CHAPTER THREE

WHEN SPEAKING OF
OTHER RELIGIONS

Growing up in a suburb of Kansas City in the 1960s and 1970s, I didn't know any Muslims, Hindus, or Buddhists. My sole exposure to people of other faiths was one Jewish friend. At that time, most Kansas City country clubs did not allow Jewish members, and a number of communities, including the one where the church I serve is located, carried deed restrictions prohibiting Jews from buying homes. It was unthinkable that a Muslim or Hindu or Buddhist might move into the neighborhood. Who determined that Jews and other religious groups should not be allowed to move into these communities or join the country clubs?

It was much easier in those days to accept unquestioningly the assumptions that people of other faiths were ignorant and misguided heathens and that they would, on Judgment Day, be consigned to hell for not having chosen the one true religion.

Fast-forward forty years. It is unthinkable that people of non-Christian religions would be prohibited from buying homes in certain neighborhoods or joining certain country clubs. If you live in an urban area, it is likely that you have at least one friend, coworker, or neighbor who is practicing a faith other than Christian. For many Christians, the more people they know who are devout members of other religions the harder it becomes to believe that all such people will suffer eternally in hell because they did not call upon the name of Jesus Christ. This is particularly true for young adults who have grown up in a more multicultural, pluralistic world than previous generations.

During his six years of service in Afghanistan and Iraq, John had been surrounded by men, women, and children who were raised in a world that is as Muslim as the United States is thought to be Christian. He saw people stop what they were doing in the middle of the day and fall to their knees in prayer; he saw their devotion to God and observed their efforts to faithfully live their scriptures. John became increasingly skeptical of Christian claims about the fate of people of other religions. In our meeting together, this is what he said about how Christians get it wrong regarding people of other faiths:

> One of the things I have always had trouble swallowing with the Christian faith is that we have a God of

compassion, a God of love, a God of forgiveness, but if you don't say "Jesus you're my savior," you're gonna burn. Flat out.... That's not forgiving, that's not compassion, that's coercion, that's blackmail. People all over the world . . . could live the best life. They could be compassionate, they could be understanding, they could do their best to help their community, to help other people, to serve their nation . . . but you're going to tell me that this person who lived an idyllic life of straight moral value is going to go to hell just because he didn't say "I love Jesus"? There's something there that is not right. There is something about that puzzle piece that doesn't fit in with what Christian faith is trying to sell.

Let's look at how Christians get it wrong regarding the theological question of the eternal fate of people of other religions, and what it might look like when Christians get it right.

Christianity That Repels

Let's clarify for a moment what we mean by people of "other faiths." In this chapter, I mean people who are adherents of a religion other than Christian. Orthodox Christians,

Roman Catholics, and Protestants all claim to be followers of Jesus Christ. They represent different sects within the Christian faith. For our purposes here, "other faiths" refers to Jews, Muslims, Hindus, Buddhists, and others.

Most Americans know very little about faiths other than their own. How much do you know about Islam, Hinduism, Buddhism, or Judaism? Here's a little pop quiz to test your knowledge:

- When do most Jews gather for worship (what day of the week and what portion of the day)?
- In what century did Mohammed die?
- Name the one Hindu scripture that is likely to be in every Hindu's home.
- When did the Buddha live?

In an informal survey of my Christian friends, few were able to answer more than one of these questions correctly.*

* (1) Most Jews gather on Friday evenings for worship—the Jewish Sabbath runs from sunset Friday to sunset Saturday. (2) Mohammed lived from 570 to 632 CE. (3) Most Hindu homes have a copy of the Bhagavad-Gita. (4) Scholars are not certain when the Buddha lived, but there is consensus that he lived 700 to 900 years after the time of Moses and 400 to 500 years before the time of Jesus. His teachings were committed to writing about the time Jesus lived.

When my older daughter was sixteen, she came to me and said, "Dad, I'm a Christian because you are a Christian. I've not studied any of the other world religions. I don't know anything about them. How can I know that Christianity is true if I've not considered any of the other faiths?" Danielle was reflecting the sentiments of many young adults today.

Her question gave me an idea. What would happen if I could lead my entire congregation in a study of four of the great religions of the world—Hinduism, Buddhism, Islam, Judaism—and then compare and contrast them with Christianity in a way that demonstrated respect and humility while honestly examining the differences between them? I spent six months preparing for this sermon series. I read the Koran, portions of the Hindu Vedas, and selections from various Buddhist writings. I interviewed leading individuals representing each of these faiths and attended their worship services and rituals. Then I announced to our congregation that I would be leading this study. Most people were excited, but some people worried that if I preached this series of sermons people might lose their faith. Some, I think, were worried about losing their own faith.

Surprisingly, I found my own Christian faith deepened by this study. As I gained understanding and appreciation for what others believe and why, my convictions about the Christian faith grew stronger. At the same time, the other faiths challenged me to be a better Christian. For instance, Muslims pray five times a day and give 2.5 percent of their income to the needy. My study of Islam led me to spend more time in prayer and to a deeper desire to give to the poor. The Hindu philosophy of non-injury helped me see love in new ways. The Buddha's existential struggles related to suffering and death gave me a deeper appreciation for the Christian doctrines of redemption and resurrection.

Several dozen people actually left our church, unsettled by these sermons, but several *hundred* people chose to become Christians after hearing how we approached these other faiths with respect and a willingness to learn from them, while honestly pointing out our differences. In addition, the entire congregation came to better understand their Muslim, Hindu, Buddhist, and Jewish friends, and we are able to talk with them with respect and appreciation.[1]

Some Christians take a very different approach to talking about other religions. A young woman wrote and described her of Christians sharing their faith while she was in college:

> My college roommate and I were invited to a party being put on by a Christian group. The party was fun, and when they invited us to their Bible study later that week, we both said sure. The Bible study was anything but fun. Almost from the start, the discussion centered on whether Jews

would get to heaven. No one in the group thought they would. In fact, several in the group spoke as though the Jews were responsible for killing Jesus. My friend finally spoke up and told them that she was Jewish. The study went downhill from there. Some were soft sell, some hard sell, but all of them tried to convince my friend to "ask Jesus into her heart." When we left that evening, I'm not sure who was more upset, her or me. Since that night I haven't had anything to do with Christians.

Pressure to accept Christ seldom leads to a desire to become a Christian. No one enjoys a high-pressure sales job. When I spoke with John, he described his feelings about Christians seeking to pressure him into becoming a Christian:

> The one thing that will set me and so many other people right on their heels is when Christians are intrusive. It's when you really start pushing for it, you know. If you are going to [help a nonbeliever find faith] it's not something they're going to come to in one conversation, so do not try to convert people in one fell swoop. You might get 1 in 100, but you're going to drive the other 99 the hell away.

There is nothing wrong with Christians sharing their faith. Jesus spoke of his message as good news—and good news should be shared. The problem is when Christians share their faith in ways that are arrogant, disrespectful, hurtful, insulting, or insensitive.

In the first century of the Christian era, Christians were a tiny minority within the Roman Empire, when most people believed in a variety of gods. Today's Christians would do well to recall how the apostles instructed early Christians to live their lives and to share their faith. The apostle Paul, in Acts 17, speaks to a group of Greek philosophers in Athens. He doesn't insult them. He looks for common ground with them. He quotes their poets. He even identifies one of the unknown gods they worship with the God of the Bible. The apostle Peter, in his first letter, offers the following counsel to Christians on how they might share their faith: "live such good lives among the pagans that . . . they may see your good deeds" (2:12 NIV). He told them to "show proper respect to everyone" (v. 17). He tells them to carry themselves with humility noting, "God opposes the proud but gives grace to the humble" (5:5). And he says, "Be compassionate and humble. . . . Always be prepared to give an answer to everyone who asks you to give the reason for the hope that you have. But do this with *gentleness* and respect" (3:8, 15; emphasis added).

The Christians in the college Bible study felt great urgency to lead the young Jewish woman to accept Christ. The urgency and the pressure they applied had something to do with their belief that if the young woman did not accept Christ then she would spend eternity in hell. They were certain that this fate awaits anyone who has not accepted Jesus Christ. Will God welcome to heaven only those who call upon the name of Jesus, regardless of those persons' character, actions, or actual love of God and neighbor? To young adults, this idea is unthinkable. They find it inconsistent with a God of justice, mercy, and love.

The Fate of Faithful, Practicing Jews, Muslims, and Hindus

Let's consider three distinct answers Christians give to the question, What is the fate of faithful, practicing Jews, Muslims, and Hindus? I mention these three groups because, in the case of Muslims and Hindus, they are the next two largest religious groups in the world, following Christianity. I mention Jews because Christians are most likely to know practicing Jews. Further I am specifically speaking of persons who seek to know, love, and serve God as they have been taught about God by their religions.

Christian Exclusivism

Christians from the conservative and evangelical traditions typically answer the question of the eternal fate of faithful Jews, Muslims, and Hindus in a way similar to what we have considered so far—such persons will be damned because they did not avail themselves of the gift of salvation offered in Jesus Christ. According to this view, human beings are born contaminated by sin. Sin separates us from God both here on earth and in eternity. A holy and righteous God cannot admit persons who are still sinful into heaven. God has provided, by the offering of his Son, salvation from sin and death. It is available to all. But one has to take hold of this salvation by trusting in Christ. Imagine a person drowning in the sea. A life preserver is tossed from a ship. The person must still take hold of the life preserver to be saved from drowning. Jesus Christ is the life preserver offered by God to all. In rejecting the life preserver, the individual is left to save herself or himself—a feat that is said to be impossible for human beings.

In the fifth century, Saint Augustine championed this view. It was restated by John Calvin in the sixteenth century. In its harshest, yet most consistent form, it excludes from heaven even infants who die who did not receive Christ. It excludes those with mental disabilities who do not receive Christ. It excludes from heaven any who have never heard the good news of Jesus Christ. Many Christians allow exceptions in these cases, but the most consistent and hard-line do not.

I spoke with an individual who holds the hard-line, exclusivist view on this issue. He was leaving our church because of the sermons I was preaching on different religions. I asked, "Are you suggesting that the Native Americans who lived on this continent for thousands of years before the first missionaries arrived were all sent to hell even though they never had the opportunity to hear of Jesus Christ? We know many of them were deeply religious and sought God. Regardless of how they lived, how much they sought God, all of them— every man, woman, and child—was destined for hell without any opportunity to even call upon the name of Jesus Christ?" He responded that this was correct, that God could have revealed his Son to them in some other way, but barring that, they were in hell.

It should be said that many evangelical Christians find the hard-line position difficult to accept; they allow exceptions. They speak of an "age of accountability" for children, before which, if they die, they are received into heaven. They say that mentally handicapped people will be judged based upon what they can understand of the grace of God. Some are willing to say the same of persons who have never heard the name of Christ. These persons will be judged based upon how they respond to God's grace as they are able to know and understand it.

Christian Universalism

A second answer to the question of the fate of faithful Jews, Muslims, and Hindus is the absolute opposite of Exclusivism. It is called *Christian Universalism* (not to be confused with the Unitarian Universalist denomination). This view suggests that all persons—not just faithful Jews, Muslims, and Hindus but all persons—will ultimately be reconciled to God and are bound for the kingdom of heaven. Christians who hold this view, who also believe in hell, think of hell as a temporary place with the primary focus of redemption rather than punishment. Hell's purpose is to lead people to repentance. Supporters of Christian Universalism claim that many of the most important theologians of the early church held this view.[2]

I like this idea, and it solves several theological problems. The challenge it poses for me is that it appears to remove human freedom to reject God, at least in the ultimate sense. The Bible teaches that God has given human beings the freedom to resist God's grace, to reject God's will, and to do what God finds abhorrent (the most obvious examples being the totalitarian dictators like Hitler, Stalin, Pol Pot, and a host of others who made themselves out to be gods and who were responsible for the murder of millions of human beings).

Christian Inclusivism

Christian Inclusivism offers a third alternative. It teaches that Jesus is the Son of God. That he came to offer salvation for the world. It teaches that the salvation of the human race is made possible by Jesus Christ. But this salvation can be given by God regardless of whether an individual personally knows Jesus Christ. God can offer this gift based upon the criteria God chooses.

This view also notes that the Christian gospel teaches that salvation is a gift given by God. Human beings do nothing to merit salvation; we simply trust in it. We receive it as a gift of God's grace. Our part is simply faith. The question, as it pertains to faithful adherents of other religions, is do they have faith? They may not have complete knowledge of what God has done in Jesus Christ, but they can nevertheless have complete trust in God. The view offers as evidence that those in the Bible who came before the time of Jesus also were saved by faith—faith that did not include Jesus Christ, for he had not yet been born (see Hebrews 11:4-40).

Inclusivism reminds us that the Christian gospel, the good news, is that we are saved by grace. In the New Testament, grace refers to God's kindness, love, care, work on our behalf, blessings, gifts, goodness, and salvation. But it is more than that—it is undeserved. God's grace is pure gift.

The apostle Paul lays out the Christian conception of how salvation works in Ephesians 2:4-5, 8-9:

> God, who is rich in mercy, out of the great love with which he loved us even when we were dead through our trespasses, made us alive together with Christ. . . . For by grace you have been saved through faith, and this is not your own doing; it is the gift of God—not the result of works, so that no one may boast.

We are saved by God's initiative, because of *God's* love, *God's* righteousness, *God's* kindness, and *God's* mercy. For those who don't understand or have not made sense of the gospel, but who have sought God—to love God, to do what God desires—the very act of seeking God is an expression of faith.

Many conservative and evangelical Christians are surprised to hear that evangelical thinker C. S. Lewis seems to have held this view. It was powerfully laid out in the last of his series of children's books, The Chronicles of Narnia. Near the end of *The Last Battle*, we find what many interpret as a mythical portrayal of Judgment Day. Jesus is portrayed as the lion, Aslan. A man is being brought before him for judgment. The man, Emeth, has spent his entire life following the false god, Tash. He was raised by his parents to worship and serve Tash. As

Emeth sees Aslan the Lion, he suddenly realizes that Tash was not god. He falls to his face, preparing for his own destruction. Here is how Emeth describes what happens next:

> He touched my forehead . . . and said, Son, thou art wel-
> come. But I said, Alas, Lord, I am no son of thine but the
> servant of Tash. He answered, Child, all the service thou
> hast done to Tash, I account as service done to me." . . .
> Then I said, "Lord, is it then true . . . that thou and Tash
> are one?" The Lion growled. . . . "It is false." I said, . . . "I
> have been seeking Tash all my days." "Beloved," said the
> Glorious One, "unless thy desire had been for me thou
> wouldst not have sought so long and so truly. For all find
> what they truly seek."[3]

A number of prominent Christians have held this view—with varying shades and gradations—including Justin Martyr in the early church; John Wesley, the founder of the Methodist movement; evangelical theologian John Stott; and most recently Billy Graham. Inclusivism is also the official position of the Roman Catholic Church and the generally accepted view of most mainline Protestants.

This is also my own view of how God will judge non-Christians who earnestly seek to know, love, and follow God in the ways they are taught. This view maintains that salvation is by and through Christ, and that it is received by faith. It makes clear that salvation is a gift from God, given not based upon human actions, nor even as a result of our theological knowledge. It is given by God, through Christ, to whomever God wishes to give it. Based upon the Gospel accounts of Jesus' ministry, God seems to desire to give salvation to all who would listen and trust in his mercy.

When I think about God's mercy toward humankind, I'm reminded of a hymn written in 1854 by Frederic Farber, "There's a Wideness in God's Mercy":

> There's a wideness in God's mercy
> like the wideness of the sea;
> there's a kindness in God's justice,
> which is more than liberty.
>
> There is welcome for the sinner,
> and more graces for the good!
>
> There is mercy with the Savior,
> there is healing in his blood.
> For the love of God is broader
> than the measure of our mind;
> and the heart of the Eternal
> is most wonderfully kind.[4]

Then Why Share the Gospel?

Whenever I share this idea of Christian Inclusivism, someone inevitably asks, "Then why should we bother to share the gospel with people, if God may save them anyway? Why have so many missionaries risked their lives to offer Christ to people who did not know him?" I usually respond with several questions of my own: Do you mean to suggest that the only reason we share the good news of Jesus Christ is that we believe God will eternally torment people in hell if we don't tell them about Jesus? Is avoiding hell the only reason to become a Christian? Is Christianity really only about getting a ticket to heaven?

I tell others about Jesus Christ not because I'm afraid God will eternally torment them in hell if I don't persuade them to accept Christ; I share Jesus Christ with others because I believe that in him we see and understand who God is and who we are meant to be. I share Christ with others because I believe he teaches us about the love, mercy, and grace of God. From him we learn sacrificial love. In him we experience forgiveness and mercy. I tell others about Christ because I believe he is the way, the truth, and the life. I tell others about Christ because he has changed my life so that the richest and most meaningful parts of my life are somehow made so by him. I share Christ with others because I want them to know that God already loves them, and that Christ offers us both the truth about God and God's will for humanity. I share Christ with others because in Christ we hear the good news of God's sacrificial love, of forgiveness of sins, and of the hope of everlasting life. But I do not share Christ because I believe God eternally torments those who love him but don't understand to call upon the name of Christ.

When Christians Get It Right

A number of persons at the church that I serve were once Hindus, Buddhists, Muslims, or Jews who have become followers of Jesus Christ. They became followers of Jesus not because we pressured them into accepting Christ. They became followers of Jesus Christ not because we spoke ill of their former faith. And they became Christians not because we made them feel small if they did not become Christians. Instead most of our members demonstrate respect, humility, and love. At their best, our members seek to listen to and learn from people of other faiths while humbly sharing their own faith.

Ali and his wife, Fay, began attending our church in 1996. Fay was a Christian; Ali was a Muslim. A very bright man,

Ali had a successful career before retiring. He attended church every Sunday with his wife because he loved her, and she loved going to church. He even volunteered each week on our bulletin-stuffing team. The people in our 7:45 a.m. service knew that Ali was a Muslim, but that did not stop them from welcoming him with open arms, inviting him to Sunday school and to join them in serving. They never pressured him to accept Christ. They listened and showed respect for his faith while humbly sharing their own.

Four years ago Fay died. I officiated at her funeral. I worried that once Fay was gone Ali might no longer attend church. But the Sunday after her funeral there he was, sitting in his normal seat. Last year Ali moved to Florida to be closer to his son. After his move he sent me an e-mail:

> Adam, I always believed in one God. Now I believe Jesus was the Son of God. I have been a very religious person in my life, but somehow I did not fit any one label. I do not like it when people push their religion on me. You never did. You accepted me as I am.

I sought to demonstrate this acceptance, love, and respect to Ali, but it was the people in worship, at Sunday school, and on the Friday bulletin-stuffing team who accepted and loved Ali.

When Christians get it right, they show respect for people of other faiths. They listen to them, learn from them, and humbly share their faith with them. They look for points of contact and commonality, as Paul did with the philosophers in Athens. They offer reasons for their faith in Jesus Christ with gentleness and respect, as Peter taught.

1. This series was later published as a book and video-based small-group study, *Christianity and World Religions* (Nashville: Abingdon Press, 2005).

2. See http://www.tentmaker.org/tracts/Universalists.html, which includes Clement of Alexandria, Origen, Athanasius, Ambrose, John Chrysostom, Eusebius, Gregory of Nyssa, and Jerome among those who held the Universalist view.

3. C. S. Lewis, *The Last Battle* (New York: HarperCollins, 1956/1984), 186–87.

4. Frederick W. Faber, "There's a Wideness in God's Mercy," *The United Methodist Hymnal* (Nashville: The United Methodist Publishing House, 1989), 121.

CHAPTER FOUR

WHEN BAD
THINGS HAPPEN

The greatest challenge to faith in God for many people is reconciling a loving God with the suffering and pain they see in the world around them. When I talked with John, the young Army Airborne Ranger who had just returned from Iraq, he described losing five of his friends in battle. Then he said, "Over the years I've looked back and I just remember thinking, you know, if there's a God that's loving and compassionate, then why did he kill my friends? When someone tells you that there's a God, he loves you, and he cares about you, and he has a plan for you—how the hell did that plan factor in when he killed five of my friends?"

This is a serious theological question—how can a good and loving God allow, or perhaps even cause, the suffering that happens in our world? Theologians speak of this as the "problem of evil" and give the line of questioning a name: *theodicy* (from the Greek *theo*—God and *dike*—justice). Every theologian and every thoughtful Christian will wrestle with this question. The purpose of this chapter is not to provide the answer to the question—though I'll suggest a line of reasoning that may be helpful. I would like to suggest that the long and commonly held assumptions about God's involvement in the affairs of our world—the things Christians say in the face of suffering, and even in the face of blessing—may be both wrong and actually serve to push people away from God. I invite Christians and non-Christians alike to question the assumptions you may have been taught regarding God's relationship to both the evil and the good that happens in our world and to ultimately get it right when it comes to how we speak about God and suffering.

Does Everything Happen for a Reason?

As I mentioned previously, a couple of years ago our church set up a blog inviting young adults to respond to the question, *When do Christians get it wrong?* One young woman posted this reply:

> Our baby died this past spring when he was six weeks old. So many Christians we have encountered since that time

tell us "this was God's plan." . . . Before this tragic event, I guess I thought this was how life worked too.. . .

But there is no way that the death of an innocent six-week-old and our inability to get pregnant again is part of some master plan. And if it is then I'm simply not interested in the God that has that plan.

Well-meaning Christians, seeking to offer comfort to this woman, had the opposite impact. They neither comforted her, nor helped her draw comfort from God. Instead, they implied that God was responsible for the death of this woman's baby. Some may find comfort in the idea that God brings about the death of six-week-old children, but most would find it difficult to worship, love, serve, and trust a God who acts in this way.

Christians often say things like "It must be the will of God" or "Everything happens for a reason." The former assumes that everything happens because God wills it to happen. The latter assumes that God has a plan in place—a predetermined script for our planet and everyone on it—and that everything that happens is written in the script and serves a purpose that we simply cannot see right now. Most people accept these assumptions without question. I invite you to question them. (At the end of this chapter I will suggest that God does have a plan, but that it may be broader than we can imagine.)

The young woman's friends sought to console her by saying that the death of her child was part of God's plan. It is unlikely that their intention was to associate her suffering with God's punishment or judgment, although that is often what we tend to do in regard to the suffering of another. Individuals going through adversity may also believe that God is punishing them. As I was talking with a man who had lost his job in the "Great Recession" of 2008–2009, he asked, "What have I done that was so bad that God is punishing me like this?" The man assumed that his job loss was God's doing, and when he could not find another job, his mind immediately moved to the idea of punishment.

Part of what this man needed was for someone to help him question his original assumption. Did the entire U.S. economy falter simply so God could punish this one man? Were all of the people who were laid off in need of God's punishment? Did God cause the economic recession that led to the loss of his job? Or was this the result of a lot of very bad economic decisions made on the part of people on both Wall Street and Main Street? These questions needed to be explored with this man.

It is worth questioning when an individual believes that some act of suffering is God's punishment. Christians really get it wrong, however, when they begin to tell others that their suffering is God's judgment.

In August 2005, Hurricane Katrina struck the Gulf Coast of the United States causing the death of more than eighteen hundred people and tens of thousands of people to lose their homes. Following the hurricane, I recall reading one man's blog about the destruction of so much of the Gulf Coast:

> Many thoughtful Americans are asking, "Why did this happen?" There is an answer to this question. . . . The answer is found in understanding that man is not in control. God is! Everything in the sky, the sea and on earth is subject to His control. . . . Was there wickedness in New Orleans, Alabama and Mississippi? Well, let's see. There was the burgeoning Gulf Coast gambling industry, with a new casino that was to open on Labor Day weekend. . . . And then there was the 34th Annual gay, lesbian and transgender . . . Labor Day gala. . . . Further, there is the well-known corruption, drugs, and immoral playground of the French Quarter.

This Christian was very clear—God sent the hurricane as an act of judgment upon the sin prevalent on the Gulf Coast. Never mind that the "immoral playground of the French Quarter" was actually spared by Katrina! Never mind that the casinos along the Gulf Coast reported their best year ever the year after they reopened. And never mind that there were thousands of Christians who lost their homes and some their lives in the destruction! This Christian was certain that God had brought Katrina to punish the heathens of New Orleans, Alabama, and Mississippi!

People of faith have struggled with viewing suffering as God's judgment since biblical times. This is how much of the Old Testament views suffering. If you suffer, it is because you have sinned. But in the middle of the Old Testament is a book that was written to counter this idea. The Book of Job is the story of a man who is righteous, and yet he suffers greatly. His friends arrive to comfort him, and at first they do a wonderful job. Here's how the book describes the scene when they first come to be with their friend:

> Now when Job's three friends heard of all these troubles that had come upon him, each of them set out from his home—Eliphaz the Temanite, Bildad the Shuhite, and Zophar the Naamathite. They met together to go and console and comfort him. When they saw him from a distance, they did not recognize him, and they raised their voices and wept aloud; they tore their robes and threw dust in the air upon their heads. They sat with him on the ground seven days and seven nights, and no one spoke a word to him, for they saw that his suffering was very great. (Job 2:11-13)

Here his friends do what friends need to do. They just sit in silence with him. They don't try to explain anything. They don't think that something they say is going to make things better. They don't presume to have all the answers; they just sit with him in silence and grieve with him.

But then after seven days of sitting with Job, his friends make their big mistake—they begin opening their mouths! And as they do, they begin to tell Job that his suffering must be his fault, that it is the judgment of God, and that he should repent. Job continues to maintain his innocence. The book ends with God chastising Job's friends and blessing Job. It provides little explanation of Job's suffering except to make the point that it was not punishment for something Job had done wrong.

Everything changes in the New Testament, where we find Jesus suffering for the sins of the world. Whatever suffering our collective sin might merit, Jesus bears it for humankind. When Christians begin to suggest that suffering is God's punishment for sin, I wonder if they are not in some sense negating the cross of Christ.

Now there is sometimes a connection between sin and suffering. But the connection is not God handing down punishment. As I read the New Testament, our punishment was taken by Jesus on the cross. When we sin, there are consequences, however. *Sin* signifies turning from God's intention for our lives; the Greek word *hamartia* was a term from archery that meant, among other things, to "miss the mark." The consequences are not punishments from God; they are the natural result of doing the wrong thing. When we cheat on our spouses, pain results. When we are caught in a lie, we lose the trust of others and we experience shame. These are natural consequences of doing the wrong thing. But Christians who evaluate the suffering of others and pronounce that it is a result of the other's sin are getting it wrong. In fact, to do so is a sin.

God the Micromanager?

Let's return to the assumption that everything happens according to the will of God.

Christians who believe that God is controlling everything often speak of God's "sovereignty." This term means that God is the highest authority, there is no one to whom God reports and no one to whom God answers. God is the Supreme Ruler—the "King of the Universe." The universe is the rightful property of God, who created it. Nearly all Christians would agree that God is sovereign—the highest authority and not dependent upon anyone or anything else.

In an attempt to glorify God, however, some people go too far. They claim that God is not only the highest authority but also the "Supreme Micromanager." They would never use this phrase to describe God, but this is what their picture of God looks like. They suggest that God is actually controlling every dimension of creation. This is sometimes referred to as "determinism." The logical outcome of this line of reasoning, as we will see, makes God a monster. Let's consider what it would mean to assume that God controls every dimension of creation.

There are approximately 75 trillion to 100 trillion cells in your body. Does God control each cell, all the time, in every one of the earth's six billion people? Does God determine at any given moment that a particular cell in this person should die, or that this cell should become cancerous? Does God determine every electrical impulse in the body and every thought in every human brain at every moment in order to control every detail of human existence? This is what would be required if God controls all of the affairs of our world.

But it doesn't stop there. In order for God to control everything, God would also need to control the billions and trillions of cells and the brain impulses in all of the trillions of other creatures on our planet; for all of creation is interconnected. Where does this stop? Does God control the properties of every molecule, atom, and electron of everything in creation at all times, dictating that this one should act this way and that one in that way? This is the only way that God could exert complete control over all things at all times in order to ensure that every event happens according to God's will. Those who define sovereignty in terms of control would need to expand God's control beyond our planet to the universe—all 150 billion galaxies like our own Milky Way and the hundreds of billions of stars like our sun that make up each of the 150 billion galaxies in our universe. On each of these and everything in between, God would control every subatomic particle at all times.

This seems a tall order, even for God. I don't suggest that God cannot do this. I believe all creation is sustained by God and draws its existence from God. But if God does exercise this kind of control, it raises a host of questions. The first is simply, why? Why would God create a universe that requires constant, moment-by-moment control? Why would God create human beings with the appearance of freedom and a longing for freedom if God is going to control every thought, every word, and every action behind the scenes? And if God controls everything we do, which implies that God also determines the outcome of all things, what is the point of exerting any effort? "*Que será, será*—what will be, will be."

This leads to another assumption—that history unfolds

according to God's predetermined plan. According to this view, God has written a story for the universe—and for each of us—that is now unfolding. We don't know how the story goes or how it ends, but God knows because God wrote the script. We have the illusion of making our own choices, but in fact we do no such thing because God has predetermined exactly what will happen, and we cannot change it. God controls all of the variables so that each person's story proceeds exactly as God intends.

This raises even more questions. For example: If God has already decided who will win the Super Bowl, and the winning and losing teams can do nothing to change the outcome, why practice, work out, or exert effort to be better prepared than one's opponent? Whatever you do you are supposed to do—any choice you make, good or evil, must be the choice God wants you to make. "*Que será, será.*"

Some people who hold these views will read this chapter and call my views heretical. If that's you, remember that, according to your own views, my writing these words must have been God's plan. According to this view, I didn't strike any of the keys on my computer keyboard of my own volition; it was the impulse of God that led me to say each of these things. So you might want to take up your argument with God. I say that in jest, but the fact is that human responsibility seems to disappear if everything we do is really ultimately what God predetermined before we were born. I have read many arguments that human beings are responsible for their actions despite the fact that God has predetermined what we will do. Personally, I have not found these arguments for determinism completely coherent.

I'm reminded of a character played by comedian Flip Wilson on television in the 1970s—the character's name was Geraldine—whose favorite phrase was "The devil made me do it." This excused Geraldine from responsibility for any wrongdoing. For hardcore preachers of determinism, the more accurate phrase would be "God made me do it."

Most people become deeply troubled by this picture of God controlling everything when they encounter horrific evil. Some years ago two drug addicts, a man and a woman, went on a rampage, videotaping their rape and murder of a number of women. They kidnapped and brutally tortured a young woman who survived the ordeal. If God has a predetermined plan for each person, and if God controls all things so that everything happens according to God's plan, then these two persons were simply doing what God foreordained. How can this be? How could a loving, just, merciful, and compassionate God plan and will this kind of evil? One might argue, "You haven't seen the tremendous good that will come of such evil. You will be able to see it one day." I believe God is able to redeem suffering and bring good from evil; but to say that God planned, willed, and prompted the hearts of those who committed such a heinous crime in order to accomplish some greater good strikes me as the worst kind of blasphemy. No ends could justify such terrible means. To claim such an act is the will of God is to say that God is neither loving nor just.

We can apply this same line of theological reasoning to every area of life, which means that every automobile accident; every epidemic outbreak; every tornado, hurricane, or earthquake; every act of corporate malfeasance; and every act of human treachery are ultimately scripted by God and occur under God's guiding hand.

I encourage you to question these assumptions about God.

I do not believe God is a micromanager or that everything happens because God wills it. In fact, one overarching message of the Bible for me is that much of what happens in the world is not God's will. From the Bible's opening story of Adam and Eve eating the forbidden fruit to its closing story of the forces of darkness waging war against God at Armageddon, human beings are repeatedly guilty of doing the opposite of what God commands.

Giving God Credit for the Good but Not Blaming God for the Bad?

Some reading this might ask: "If you say that God is not responsible for the bad things that happen, why give God credit for the good things that happen?" This is a great question. How can Christians credit God for the good things while saying that God is not also responsible for the bad? If God is not responsible for the bad things that happen in life, why should we say that God is responsible for the good things?"

These are important questions. Let's consider examples that help illustrate the theological problem and why the language of many Christians, even when it comes to the good things, can turn thinking people away from God.

A wide receiver scores a touchdown in an NFL game and then points to the heavens and makes the sign of the cross. What is the message? If the player is saying, "God, I recognize that you are the source of my life, and I am grateful for you and the opportunities I have and I wish to honor you," that's okay. But if he is pausing to suggest that God orchestrated the touchdown, we would do well to question this line of reasoning. Is God the "12th Man" on the field, playing with whichever team God favors? What does that mean for the other team? Does God help one team or another win? Wouldn't we call that cheating?

A popular television preacher suggested that God had blessed him with a parking space in the front row of the mall parking lot. He paused to thank God for freeing up the space on such a busy day. This was, to him, simply a sign of God's goodness and blessings. Once more I question the assumptions behind this prayer of thanks. Does God provide front row parking spaces for some, while thousands of others die each day in automobile accidents?

A man escapes unharmed from a building felled in Port-au-Prince in the 2010 earthquake. He stands before a reporter in front of the building and declares his gratitude that God saved him. Behind him stands a man looking over the rubble. His young daughter is buried and presumed dead inside. If God delivered the man before the microphone, why did God not deliver the little girl?

We might ask if God delivered the man, or if the man was just fortunate. I don't know. Is it possible that God miraculously intervened to save this man? Yes. It may be that God has some purpose we cannot perceive in saving this man.

When I was sixteen years old, I drove my old Ford Maverick forty-five miles per hour down a damp road. A truck was coming from the opposite direction. As the truck and I were passing, a car that had been tailgating the truck decided to pull across the street into a car wash. The driver pulled right in front of me; I had no time to stop. I slammed on my brakes and broadsided her car. These were the days before seat belt laws and I was not wearing my seat belt. Everything in my car was hurled forward at forty-five miles per hour, striking the windshield or wedging into and under the dash and getting thrown out the windows. My car was totaled, but I distinctly remember feeling something like hands holding me in place against the seat. I didn't bang my head against the windshield, and I was completely unharmed (as was the driver of the other car).

I believed then, and still believe, that God spared my life that day. I believed that there was something God wished me to accomplish. In the years since, however, I have always worn my seat belt. I don't know if I have already accomplished whatever God intends for me; I assume that next time I might not feel those hands holding me in place! Having offi-ciated at a number of funerals for people who died in car crashes, I know that most people in collisions like the one I was in do not survive.

Back to the man from Haiti. He may have been saved by God for some purpose yet to be fulfilled. But most people who are in a building during an earthquake, or who are in a collision going forty-five miles per hour without a seat belt, will not have that experience. Does that mean God predetermined that they should suffer while others are spared?

Let's look at one more illustration that invites us to consider God's ordinary ways of working in our lives and how we might give thanks for these things.

Consider the thanksgiving given at mealtime. When we sit down to eat supper, my wife and I always pause to thank God for the meal we are about to receive. What are we thanking God for in this meal? After all, farmers grew the lettuce and tomatoes and other vegetables. These foods did not miraculously appear at our table. Truckers brought this food to our market. Employees at the store stocked the produce aisle. My wife prepared the food with the help of the people at the power company. So what are we thanking God for? We thank God for a world that supplies such delicious things, for the blessing of taste and the joy of eating, for farmers and truckers and grocery store stockers, and for life itself—all of these are results of God's creative and sustaining work. It is in this sense that Christians rightly give thanks for everything; not because God is the *immediate* cause of all good, but because God is the *ultimate* cause of these blessings.

Does God Have a Plan?

There are so many more things that can and should be said about God's providence—how God works in our world. As I was writing this chapter my wife said, "That topic is an entire book, not just one chapter," and she was right. I do not hope or presume in this chapter to provide all of the answers to perhaps the greatest theological question of all time. The truth is, I don't have it all sorted out myself. But I want to end with a word about what I believe is God's plan, and then one final example of God's relationship to suffering and when I've seen Christians get it right.

I do believe God has a plan for our lives, but not one written in stone that God forces us to follow. Much of God's plan is fairly simple to understand. We read the Scriptures, particularly the teachings of Jesus, and we seek to follow them. In every situation, in every encounter, in every relationship, and in every decision, we seek to express the love of God, the love of neighbors, and what is just.

At the same time each of us has unique gifts and abilities and perhaps places of influence, and God's will is that we use these to do God's work. At times God places on our hearts a special call or a particular opportunity. We need to listen and say yes. But even when we have not heard or discerned a particular call, we know the teachings of Jesus about God's will and plan for our lives.

I find that each day God leads us, if we are paying attention and listening. I often feel prompted to make a call or to go here or there, and often when I pay attention to these prompts, I find myself having a conversation with someone who needed a pastor at just that moment. I may bump into someone who has been struggling and needs care. We speak of these things, not as mere coincidences, but as "God-incidents." The challenge and task are to pay attention and to listen to the whisper of God.

These God-incidents often seem to happen when I'm on airplanes. I've learned to pay attention. I was flying from San Antonio to Dallas a few weeks after the 2010 earthquake in Haiti. I had been in Port-au-Prince just a week earlier to meet with church leaders and to survey the damage so that our church could develop a strategy for early response. I sat in an aisle seat. There was an empty seat and then there was a woman sitting at the window. I looked over at her and saw that she was crying. I asked if she was okay, and she said she was just thinking about her mom, whose birthday she was flying to Dallas to celebrate. She said, "I was just thinking about how much I love her."

We struck up a conversation about our parents and our children. Somehow the conversation turned to Haiti, and I told her I had just been there. Then she asked the question that usually signals the end of a conversation: "What do you do for a living?" I told her I was a pastor and she said, "Oh," in a somewhat hesitant tone. I thought that might be the end of the conversation. But a few minutes later she turned and said, "Can I ask you a question?"

"Of course, anything," I replied.

She asked, "How do you reconcile a loving God with the terrible devastation that happened in Port-au-Prince?" I sensed she had been thinking about this, and that she was asking this earnestly. This is what I told her:

"Let me first say that I don't believe God caused this earthquake. It was not meant to teach the Haitians or to punish them. We have a pretty good idea why earthquakes happen—it is not the Bible but science that helps us here." Several years ago I spent time studying the latest theories about earthquakes. I shared my understanding about them with her: "Earthquakes are the result of a process that actually cools the core of our planet, produces mountain ranges, and creates the earth's magnetic fields. Under the surface of the earth, magma is superheated at the core; it rises like hot air and then spreads and cools as it comes closer to the surface of the earth. As it spreads it carries the earth's plates, moving them. The magma cools, falls back toward the core, reheats and rises again, continuing the movement of the earth's plates. The plates rub against one another, eventually getting stuck. When the plates finally break free they release massive amounts of energy. This process appears to be essential for life on our planet."

She seemed very interested. I continued, "Port-au-Prince lies on one of those places where the plates were stuck. The damage was exacerbated by the fact that this is a very poor nation and buildings were not constructed to withstand this kind of earthquake. When human beings collide with the powerful forces of nature that allow life to be sustained on our planet, nature always wins. When you add poverty to the equation, the results are catastrophic."

I continued, "So, the question is really, where was God in Port-au-Prince when the earthquake occurred? God wasn't shaking the earth in order to kill innocent people. But I saw God in a medical team from a church in Iowa, treating people in the midst of the rubble. I saw God in the doctors and rescue workers, who were moved by the tragedy and immediately left the comfort of their homes in the States to be of help. I saw God in the people in the caravan of semi trucks loaded with food and supplies traveling between Santo Domingo and Port-au-Prince.

"God was the source not of the earthquake but of the comfort and hope people found as they buried their dead. On Wednesday night, while our team was in Port-au-Prince, there was another earthquake, and from the makeshift tents you could hear people cry out in fear. But then they quickly broke into the singing of hymns. God was their comfort and strength. For those who lost loved ones, God is the only hope that they will see their children or parents or friends again. I saw God in the generosity of my congregation who gave hundreds of thousands of dollars to aid the victims."

And then I concluded, "If you take God out of the equation in Haiti, you still have an earthquake with 200,000 people dead, but you have just removed the single most important source of comfort and hope."

She responded, "I'm Jewish, and that is the best answer I've ever heard. Thank you. That gives me hope."

Christians get it wrong when they attribute tragedy to the will, plan, and hand of God. They get it wrong when they blame victims as the cause of their own suffering. But they get it right when they walk with those undergoing suffering, and when they selflessly serve their neighbors in need. In this way they become the hands and feet and voice of God, caring for God's children in their moment of need.

CHAPTER FIVE

IN DEALING WITH HOMOSEXUALITY

The 2007 Barna study, released as the book *unChristian* and described in Chapter One, found that 91 percent of young adults labeled Christianity "anti-homosexual," and this perception led many young adults to turn away from the church. This finding was substantiated in our interviews with and input from young adults at the Church of the Resurrection. John raised the issue, unsolicited, in our conversation:

> It applies a little bit more to my generation than it does to previous generations . . . issues on homosexuality. I myself am not, but at the same time, I fully support those who do choose it as their lifestyle, and for people in our generation, you know, homosexuality wasn't something that was spoken of in hushed tones, about people in back alleys. Some people were exposed to the "it's a crime against God" and "you'll burn in hell" aspect of it, but for many people in this day and age, my age or younger, we've seen it in the

media, in our schools, in our communities, and it has become something that is accepted. You know, for a vast majority of people in my generation, people might not be homosexual, they might not even like the thought of homosexuality, but I know [that] almost all of the guys I've talked to about it have said, yeah, I don't see anything that's wrong with it. And trying to do things in the political process like ban gay marriage on a religious basis, trying to tell people that they're not eligible for the same rights of a man and woman just because it's man and man, to me that's just like looking at a biracial couple and saying you can have a legal union, but you can't have a marriage because one of you is black and one of you is white, and there was a day and age when that was considered a crime against God.

John captured well the sentiments of many young adults. I found it particularly interesting to hear these comments from a man who had just spent six years as an Army Airborne Ranger, given that, at the time, the military and the church were among only a handful of organizations that would not hire self-avowed homosexuals.

A 2010 Pew Forum study noted what we have known for some time: young adults see homosexualiy very differently from those who came before them. Of people born after

63 percent felt that homosexuality should be accepted by society, while only 35 percent of those over 65 years of age believed it. Even among "evangelicals," 39 percent of young adults indicated that homosexuality should be accepted. When asked if homosexual relations are always wrong, 78 percent of Baby Boomers said yes (down from a high of 88 percent among this generation twenty years ago). Forty-three percent of young adults said homosexual relations are always wrong.[1]

Division over this issue is the present reality. It's true in society as a whole, in the mainline denominations, in my own congregation, and even among our staff and pastors. In fact, many thoughtful Christians find themselves conflicted, searching for the right take on an issue that has great complexity. We struggle with Scripture, and with whether what we read there regarding same-sex intimacy reflects God's eternal and timeless will or the cultural suppositions of the time in which the biblical texts were written.

Often the debate is presented as an argument about the authority of the Bible. There are those who say that if you see biblical references to same-sex intimacy as culturally bound and no longer binding today, you are rejecting the authority of the Bible. I don't believe this. The issue is not biblical authority, but biblical interpretation.

As one studies the New Testament, it becomes clear that Christians have, from the beginning, recognized that certain scriptural commands were no longer binding. Deeply held convictions based upon unambiguous commands of the Bible were set aside by the early church. Bear in mind that their only Bible was the Old Testament; the New Testament had yet to be written. Yet they looked at passages about circumcision (which preceded the law of Moses), dietary laws, ritual laws, and so many others, and they indicated that these were no longer binding upon believers.

In Acts 10, Peter, who is hungry, is praying intently as he waits for his meal to be prepared. He has a vision in which a bedsheet is lowered from heaven. On the sheet are animals—mammals, birds, and reptiles that his Bible, the Old Testament, clearly and repeatedly forbids him to eat. As a good Jew, he has followed that rule faithfully all his life.

But then he hears the voice of the Lord say, "Take and eat." God is telling him to do something expressly prohibited by Jewish law, to eat what had been declared unclean.

"Surely not, Lord!" he says, "for nothing profane or unclean has ever entered my mouth."

But the Lord responds, "Do not call impure anything that God has made clean."

Then, servants of a Roman soldier named Cornelius come to his door and take him to their master's home, where he eats with Cornelius and his friends, all of whom are uncircumcised Gentiles. In those days, doing so was absolutely scandalous; Jewish law forbade eating with people who were unclean. Peter shared the gospel with them, and the Holy Spirit came upon them. Peter baptized these uncircumsised Gentiles into the Christian faith.

Along the way, Peter had an epiphany. He suddenly understood: *The rules are changing!* He said to the people in Cornelius's home, "You yourselves know that it is unlawful for a Jew to associate with or to visit a Gentile, but God has shown me that I should not call anyone profane or unclean."

So, even Peter, who spent three years with Jesus himself, struggled with the Bible and with a God who seemed to be saying that what was written in the Scripture and what the people had interpreted might not actually be God's will.

Slavery, Women, and Sexuality

Through the centuries, many followers of Jesus have contended with the Scripture as Peter did, and we do so today. The Bible is a document both divine and human. Christians do not believe, as Muslims do about the Koran, that God dictated the Bible word-for-word to its human authors. We know many of those authors' names. We learn of their character as we read their words. They were people who had a deep faith in God, and at the same time they heard and understood God in the light of their culture and times. The Bible is the timeless, inspired word from God found within the writings and reflections of very human authors. This means that we find things in the Bible that made sense at the time to the authors, but may not make sense, or even be applicable, to us today. We find areas where both Christians and non-Christians struggle with what we find in the Bible. For Peter, it was a word about what was clean and unclean. For us, there are things such as slavery, the role of women, and sexuality.

There are 326 verses in the Bible that refer to slaves and slavery. One of the laws Moses said God gave to him states clearly that "the slave is the owner's property." Today we see slavery, owning another person, as unjust and immoral. If we're going to take the Bible seriously, we have to ask: Do these verses about slavery represent God's timeless will, or do they represent the culture in which the Bible was written? Later, in the New Testament, both Paul and Peter are clear that slaves were to be submissive to their masters, even masters who were cruel, and to obey them "with fear and trembling." Those passages were used to perpetuate the slave trade in America.

Early in Genesis, we are told that the woman would be ruled over by her husband because Eve had convinced Adam to eat the forbidden fruit. The law of Moses decrees that women are worth half of what men are worth when they are "redeemed." The law allowed wives to be counted as part of the husband's property . Fathers were allowed to sell their daughters into slavery or give them to other men to be wives. In the New Testament, Paul affirms that women should submit to their husbands and remain silent in church.

When I hear people say they want a return to the Bible's sexual ethics I think, "Really?" The Old Testament condones polygamy, concubines, and the forcing of slaves to sleep with their master in order to bear him children. Do these practices represent God's timeless will for sexual ethics? I hope not.

But those were not the last words on the subject. In the New Testament, we find slave traders identified as evil, and Paul notes that in the gospel there is neither slave nor free. Though slave owners in the young church were not told to set their slaves free, they were cautioned to treat them justly. It took 1700 years for Christians finally to question seriously the New Testament's tacit approval of slavery. Wilberforce, Wesley, and others began to condemn the practice on the basis of a broader message of Scripture— that all human beings were created in the image of God, and that the buying, selling, and owning of human beings was incompatible with justice. They, like Peter, came to recognize that what was written in the law and accepted in the New Testament was not necessarily God's timeless will for humanity.

We also find in Scripture another view of women. In the first creation story, women are created in the image of God alongside men. The Song of Solomon affirms great love for a woman. Proverbs 31 lifts up an ideal woman. When we come to the New Testament, we see Jesus standing against the culture by ministering to women and elevating their role. We find Paul saying that husbands should love their wives as Christ loved the church and gave himself up for her. Thank God that today we see women as equal partners in ministry and valued by God. But for nineteen centuries the church, through her unwillingness to recognize the role of culture in shaping the New Testament, played a role in keeping women subordinate to, and often repressed by, men.

When it comes to sexual matters, there are passages that I believe do capture God's timeless will—passages that forbid adultery, sexual immorality, and promiscuity. So, on what basis do we decide that some things are still binding and others are not? I suggest that we decide this by evaluating passages in the light of Jesus' two great commandments: love God with all that you are, and love your neighbor as yourself. Passages that would lead us to hurt others, break covenant in our relationships, or make us slaves to our sex drives are not consistent with the command to love our neighbor, and therefore they are not binding upon us. For passages that do not violate the great commandments we may at least ask: Do these reflect God's timeless will, or do they reflect the presuppositions and values of the humans who wrote them?

Understanding that Scripture contains both the timeless will of God and the timebound cultural presuppositions of its authors has led me to ask this question: Is it possible that the passages relating to homosexuality in the Bible are in the same category as those related to these other subjects?"

The Bible and Same-Sex Relationships

And so we arrive again at the issue of biblical authority vs. biblical interpretation. Most Christians on both sides of the question of homosexuality believe in the authority of the Bible. I read my Bible every morning and study it ten to fifteen hours a week. I strive, like Wesley, to be a "man of one book." No book has a greater impact upon my life. Its words reflect my deepest convictions and highest aspirations. I hear God speaking to me as I read it. The question is not whether I believe in biblical authority; the question is how I *interpret* the Scripture.

There are eight passages of Scripture related to same-sex activity, but let me say that I don't think two of them have anything to do with homosexuality. These two passages are in Genesis chapter 19 and Judges chapter 19, and they are parallel stories of the gang rape of strangers by men who likely would not have considered themselves homosexual. These stories are about torturing and demonstrating power over strangers—dehumanizing them. The stories have nothing to do with a loving relationship between two people of the same sex. Likewise, in verse 7 of the Book of Jude, there is a reference to Sodom, from the Genesis 19 story. For the reasons just stated, this passage is not about same-sex loving relationships.

So we are left with five verses in the Bible related to same-sex intimacy. Two of these are in Leviticus, where they are included in what scholars call the "holiness code." There, we find verses that say you should not plant two different kinds of seed in the same field and should not blend fabrics or mix clean and unclean animals, because those things are abnormal. But we also find commandments telling us to love our neighbor and prohibiting incest. As we read the holiness code, we find things about which we can say, "Yes, that's meaningful for us today," and other things about which it's obvious that, "No, this doesn't represent God's timeless will for us." Once again, every Christian interprets and then sets aside some of these verses, while retaining others. I know of no Christians who believe God demands that we not wear blended fabrics.

It is in the holiness code that we read, "If a man lies with a male as with a woman, both of them have committed an abomination; they shall be put to death; their blood is upon them" (Leviticus 20:13). Regardless of where you stand on the issue of same-sex intimacy, do you think this verse captures the timeless will of God? Is it God's will that gay and lesbian people be put to death? Few Christians would suggest that this punishment should be applied to gay and lesbian people, so they have already determined that a portion of this Scripture should be set aside.

If we agree that we shouldn't put gay and lesbian people to death, then aren't we saying that at least part of that verse is more a reflection of Israel's views on homosexuality than of God's timeless will? Even if we think the first part of the verse has meaning for us today, doesn't that mean we already are trying to sort through which part is and which part isn't in each of these categories of Scripture?

The next of the verses related to same-sex intimacy in the Bible are in Paul's letter to the Romans. Jesus doesn't talk about same-sex attraction, but Paul says, "For this reason God gave them up to degrading passions. Their women exchanged natural intercourse for unnatural, and in the same way also the men, giving up natural intercourse with women, were consumed with passion for one another. Men committed shameless acts with men and received in their own persons the due penalty for their error" (Romans 1:26-27).

Paul is clearly echoing Leviticus, describing what is normal and what is abnormal, what is natural and what is unnatural. I have no doubt that for Paul the idea of a man being with a man was unnatural. It seemed unclean. It just seemed wrong. And when he looked at the culture around him, what he saw as expressions of homosexuality were things that you and I would also see as wrong. He saw older men who took younger boys as their playthings. He saw the temple prostitutes, male and female, engaged in prostitution. He saw people who were living lives totally given over to their sex drives.

There were plenty of places where he could point and say, "Look how absolutely wrong this is." Paul had no conception of the kinds of things some of us are just beginning to understand—that while perhaps 95 percent of the population may be wired to have an attraction toward the opposite sex, there may be five percent who by nature or nurture feel they are different. That five percent, by the time they are older, are drawn to love people of the same sex. It's clear that Paul couldn't see two people of the same sex living as a family together for the rest of their lives, the way he couldn't see that slavery was wrong or that women could speak in church.

The final two passages related to same-sex intimacy in the

Bible are 1 Corinthians 6:9-10, which may refer primarily to male prostitutes and those who frequented them, and 1 Timothy 1:9-10, which refers to those who lie with men as with women, again echoing Leviticus. Once more it is appropriate to ask: Are these verses like the hundreds of passages permitting slavery and the dozens suggesting that women are subordinate to and of lesser worth than men; or are they more like verses that command us to love God and neighbor, to do unto others as we would have them do unto us, and to do justice and love kindness? In other words, are describing Paul's understanding of sexual norms, or do they describe God's timeless will?

Asking the Tough Questions

Some people are crystal clear as to which category they fall into—seeing the verses as timeless, or viewing them as timebound—while other people are still trying to decide how they feel. As I have thought through the issue over the last thirty years, it has become less clear, not more. The truth is that almost all of us know someone—a friend, family member, neighbor, or co-worker—who is gay or lesbian. How does God look at these people?

I have often felt the way Peter felt, as he tried to sort out what the Bible taught about eating unclean animals or dining with with unclean Gentiles, while at the same time God was asking him to "take and eat" that which had been considered unclean and dine with Gentiles who had been considered unclean.

I came to Christ in a church where the idea was "The Bible says it, I believe it, and that settles it." That was pretty much the way I felt for years. But the more I studied the Bible, the more it became clear to me that there are many passages we don't accept as normative for us today, including those related to women, slavery, and some sexual ethics of ancient times. As I engaged the Bible in light of these questions, I began to see that the book is more complex and nuanced than I had ever thought.

Peter was unnerved at first to see that God was doing something new, such as including people in the kingdom who had previously been excluded. And I have, in the thirty years of my ministry, come to be open to the possibility that God's perspective on homosexuality may be different from what we read in Leviticus and in Paul's letter to the church at Rome. I have come to believe that God's compassion and understanding toward persons who don't fit these norms—whose fundamental wiring seems oriented toward same-sex attraction—are undoubtedly greater than the Scriptures indicate.

God's Love of People

My new understanding of the nature of Scripture opened the door for me to see this issue differently than I once had, but it was when I began to know and care about people who are homosexual that my views began to expand. I pastor a congregation of 17,000 people. If we say that persons with same-sex attractions make up perhaps five percent of the population, there may be 850 people in the congregation I serve who are homosexual. Add to this the people who have family members who are gay or lesbian, and the number of people concerned about this issue increases significantly. One Sunday I asked the members of our congregation to raise a hand if they had a family member, close friend, or someone they cared about who was homosexual. Nearly everyone raised a hand.

I think of Mary, whose pastor I have been since she was two years old. She's a sweet, kind, and humble young woman who grew up in our children's program, participated in our youth program, and is now attending college. She told me recently she is homosexual. I was moved to tears as I read some things that other Christians had told her. I think of Aaron, who grew up in our youth group, served as a church leader, and was quite serious about following Jesus Christ. I think of Kristin, whom I watched grow up. She is now a schoolteacher and in a covenant relationship with her partner.

Many of my questions about homosexuality are yet to be answered. There are dimensions of the discussion that don't fit neatly into the arguments of the Right or the Left. But I am certain of one thing—I don't want to lead a church that turns away young adults such as Mary, Aaron, and Kristin.

There are many things about Jesus that I love. One of them is that he consistently put people before rules. He had a heart for people whom others deemed sinful. He went out of his way to touch those who were unclean, and in him they found hope and love. The Pharisees were incensed that Jesus met and ate with "sinners and tax collectors." Even the disciples were a bit surprised by some of the people with whom Jesus associated. For Jesus, however, people came before rules.

One of my favorite stories of Jesus' ministry is found in John 4:5-39. Jesus waits at a well in Samaria and talks with a woman. You may want to read this story. It speaks volumes about Jesus' character and heart toward people whom others would shun. The woman has been married and divorced five times, and at this point she's living with a man who is not her husband. This was quite scandalous in the first century. Jesus speaks to her and offers her "living water"(v. 10) so that she will "never be thirsty" (v. 14). He doesn't lecture her on the evils of divorce or cohabitation. He doesn't even say, "Leave the man you are living with." He offers her grace. In response, the woman becomes the first missionary and evangelist to the

Samaritans, and we read in verse 39: "Many Samaritans from that city believed in him because of the woman's testimony."

This discussion and story lead me to an e-mail I received a couple of years ago that describes what I think it looks like when Christians get it right regarding homosexuality:

> I am a lesbian who has a partner and three children. I have never been to your church. But this e-mail is not about being gay or about the church's stance on being gay. It is about one of your members whose name is Carol. Carol lives next door to me. She was one of the first neighbors to come and say "hello." She was warm and inviting and one day she invited us to church. . . . I told her I was gay, and she didn't raise an eyebrow or frown. . . . I checked out your church's Web site and was impressed that the church was talking about this issue and not just praying it would go away.
>
> I have never valued a church by the number of people in the pews or the amount of money in the offering. What I am moved by is a woman so touched by your church that she came into my heart. . . . She opens up her home to people in need. She checks on those who aren't feeling well. And she shared Christ with a woman she knew was gay because it was in her heart to do it. I have been truly blessed by this woman, and I am hoping to visit your church in the future.

Not all Christians see the issue of homosexuality in the same way. The church is divided on this issue. But even in a divided church, we can agree that we wish to be the kind of church in which men and women who are gay and lesbian find the warmth and welcome and love of Jesus Christ. I think Christians get it wrong when they speak in ways that bring harm and alienation to God's gay children; I think we get it right when, even in our uncertainty, we express the love and welcome of the One who offered living water to the woman at the well.

I'll end with a prophecy of sorts. I am convinced that churches twenty years from now will see this issue very differently from the way most do today. I don't mean only mainline churches, but also "evangelical" churches. Why am I so sure? Because a large number of young adults in conservative and evangelical churches, as well as mainline churches, see this issue differently from their parents. They take the Bible seriously, and they understand that it contains verses that reflect the culture and times in which the Bible was written, rather than the timeless will of God. Increasingly, churches that are unwilling to see this issue with greater compassion and love will lose an entire generation of young adults whose views on homosexuality look very different from that of their parents.

1. Pew Research Center's Forum on Religion & Public Life. "Religion in the Millenniel Generation," February 2010.

CHAPTER SIX

WHEN CHRISTIANS
GET IT RIGHT

C hristians have always struggled to "get it right." Most of the New Testament was written to Christians who were "getting it wrong." They struggled with self-righteousness, hypocrisy, judgmentalism, spiritual pride, moral compromise, and a host of other issues. The New Testament letters were often aimed at correcting these things.

Underlying all of the other counsel the apostles gave for how Christians can get it right is one common refrain: To get it right is to love. Peter says it this way, "Love covers a multitude of sins" (1 Peter 4:8). James writes, "You do well if you really fulfill the royal law according to the scripture, 'You shall love your neighbor as yourself'" (James 2:8). John is even bolder in his first epistle, "Whoever does not love does not know God, for God is love" (1 John 4:8).

Among the most dysfunctional churches in the New Testament, where Christians were getting it wrong, was the church at Corinth in Greece. Their church was fractured and filled with Christians who acted in ways that scarcely resembled the Christ they claimed to follow. To these Christians, Paul writes very directly:

> If I speak in the tongues of mortals and of angels, but do not have love, I am a noisy gong or a clanging cymbal. And if I have prophetic powers, and understand all mysteries and all knowledge, and if I have all faith, so as to remove mountains, but do not have love, I am nothing. (1 Corinthians 13:1-2)

Paul goes on to describe this love that Christians are to live out:

> Love is patient; love is kind; love is not envious or boastful or arrogant or rude. It does not insist on its own way; it is not irritable or resentful; it does not rejoice in wrongdoing, but rejoices in the truth. It bears all things, believes all things, hopes all things, endures all things.
>
> Love never ends. . . . And now faith, hope, and love abide, these three; and the greatest of these is love. (1 Corinthians 13:4-8a, 13)

Why does Paul place such strong emphasis on love? Because if you boiled down the gospel to one word, it would be love. Jesus commands his disciples to love God with their entire being and to love their neighbors as they love themselves (see Luke 10:27). This is what biblical scholar Scot McKnight calls "the Jesus Creed." Jesus goes on to tell his disciples that the world will know that they are his disciples by their love (John 13:34-35). They are to love one another, to love their neighbor, to love those in need, and even to love their enemies.

Even as I write these words, I realize how often I fall short of them.

When Christians get it right, they practice sacrificial love. That is a powerful witness. It has the capacity to change the world.

When John came to me with his frustrations concerning the Christian faith, I did not argue with him. I listened to him and actually agreed with him. Many of the things that frustrated him also frustrated me. Others were things of which I had been guilty.

As I have addressed these various issues with Christians, some people get defensive. Others nod their heads. Some want to argue theology, while others say, "That's what I've always thought."

It is important to note that Christians don't have a corner on the market when it comes to getting things wrong. Muslims, Jews, Hindus, and Buddhists have gotten it wrong.

Atheists and agnostics get it wrong in many of the same ways Christians get it wrong. Getting it wrong is not simply a function of theology but of our psychology, our sociology, and ultimately of our human condition. Christians call this condition sin though you may have another name for it. We are all afflicted with the tendency to get it wrong. The seven deadly sins are universal temptations, not unique to Christians—lust, gluttony, greed, indifference, hurting others, envy, and pride—we all struggle with these temptations.

That leads me to another point. Christianity is about forgiveness, not perfection. Jesus was unnerving to the religious elite because he spent most of his time with "sinners." Of course, both the priests and the prostitutes were sinners. The difference was that the prostitutes knew they were sinners; the priests acted as though they were not. It seems clear in reading the Gospels that between sexual sins and religious hypocrisy Jesus considered religious hypocrisy far more deadly.

It should be no surprise that Christians sometimes get it wrong—Christianity doesn't invite perfect people to join up. It invites people who are prone to get it wrong and then offers them grace. As one person told me, "If I never got it wrong, I would not need Christianity!"

It's important, however, for Christians to remember that the Christian spiritual life—the life of discipleship—does not stop at forgiveness. The aim of the Christian life is to get it right. Theologians call this process *sanctification*—a word that means to be made holy. What does holiness look like? It looks like love. Over time, Christians should become more loving if we are growing in our faith. The proof of maturing in the Christian faith is not found in how much of the Bible people have memorized or how systematic their theology is. It is not even how well they avoid the more obvious sins. The proof of spiritual growth is found in the practice of love.

All Christians get it wrong some of the time, but I have had the joy of watching many Christians working to get it right.

Some time ago Vincent began attending our church. He's a gifted vocalist in his thirties who sang heavy metal and classic rock for years. Vincent is also afflicted with Tourette's syndrome. His form of Tourette's is known as coprolalia, and includes the spontaneous utterance of words that most people suppress—swear words. Vincent was diagnosed when he was an adolescent. From that time on he had felt unwelcome in church. We have a large sanctuary, but it was easy to tell when Vincent was present, starting with his first visit. As I was preaching he would blurt out swear words. It was a little unnerving at first. Some with children who did not understand what was happening moved to another part of the sanctuary. But almost instantly some people realized that Vincent had

Tourette's. When Vincent showed up for worship, a group of people sat near him and reassured him it was okay. Vincent thought that perhaps it would help if people knew his story, so one weekend we told his story and then invited him to sing. When he was finished singing about his life, the congregation rose to their feet in a standing ovation that lasted for several minutes. What they were saying to Vincent was, "We love you. We want you here. You are a gift from God!"

As they stood applauding I saw the church as it is meant to be, a community of people who welcome others with genuine love. They got it right.

Chuck, one of our members, told me a story about two other congregations who got it right. It was June 18, 1999. Chuck, his wife, Angie, and their two little boys were driving down I-24, between Jasper and South Pittsburg, Tennessee, on their way to visit Angie's folks. Chuck started to change lanes, noticed a car in his blind spot, and pulled the steering wheel back. As he did he lost control of the car and it spun around several times, then rolled over, crushed Angie's side of the car, and rolled over two more times before stopping. When the car finally came to a standstill, Chuck quickly looked to the backseat. The boys were fine, but crying. Then Chuck looked over at Angie. He could see she was unconscious and bleeding. He struggled to remove her seat belt. Within minutes the ambulance arrived. Angie and Chuck were taken in two separate ambulances to the hospital. Sometime later the chaplain from the hospital came to speak with Chuck. He told her that Angie had not survived the accident.

The chaplain had called the pastors of the two Baptist churches nearby—in Jasper and Pittsburg. Soon the pastor from Jasper, the pastor's wife from Pittsburg, and a group of laypeople were there at the hospital. Some had taken off from work to come and help. They went to the store to replace the bloodstained clothes Chuck was wearing and bought an overnight change of clothes for him and the boys. They brought toys and diapers and kept the kids while the pastor and others sought to comfort and care for Chuck. Chuck told me that eleven years later he is still overwhelmed by the generosity and love he felt from these Christians toward a stranger from Kansas. The folks from these two churches in Jasper and Pittsburg got it right that night.

Chris and his wife, Tammi, a remarkable young couple I know, moved from the suburbs to one of the most crime-ridden neighborhoods in Kansas City. Drive-by shootings, sexual assault, and drug houses are a nearly daily part of life in their community. But they felt called to move there to bring hope to the children and youth who live there. They started the Hope Center, which is seeking to transform the neighborhood and the children there. Today hundreds of people are finding hope through the education programs, medical clinic, and youth groups Chris and Tammi have launched. Chris and Tammi are Christians who get it right.

I have watched as people do the most giving and sacrificial things caring for one another in the church. Lori's husband, Jerry, was 1,000 miles away at M. D. Anderson Cancer Center where he was battling cancer. She was trying to care for her children, hold herself together, and give hope to her husband. She described her friends who mowed the yard, watched her children, assembled a playground in the backyard at midnight on Christmas Eve, and flew to Houston to be with her to help her and her husband through the crisis.

She told me she did not know how she could have made it without this care. That's what it looks like when Christians get it right.

There was Amy, who saw a young, pregnant teenager leaving McDonald's without a winter coat on a cold Kansas City evening. Amy ran to her car, got her own coat, and gave it to the girl, beginning a relationship with a teenage mother who needed a friend.

There was David, who saw a young man in a suit walking home from work in the rain. He stopped to give him a ride and discovered the young man walked two miles each way to work in the only suit he owned. The next morning David dropped off a bicycle and began a relationship with the young man that culminated in the young man receiving a scholarship to go to college.

Greg used the influence of his construction company to help break down racial barriers in Kansas City. Danielle and JT spent the first year of their married life in South Africa seeking to serve people in extreme poverty. Karla leads hundreds of people in visiting the forgotten people—the nursing home residents no one else ever visits at thirty area nursing homes. I think of the many people who volunteer in our Matthew's Ministry, serving more than one hundred special-needs children, youth, and adults and providing respite for their parents. They give up their weeknights and weekends to throw parties, lead groups, and to love our special-needs members. These are all Christians who get it right.

I could fill a lengthy book with stories like this. I'm not suggesting that only Christians do these things. I know others who do the same. But in my travels to Honduras and Haiti, to Zambia and South Africa, to the Gulf Coast after Hurricane Katrina and to the inner city in Kansas City, nearly all of the people I have met doing humanitarian work are Christians. Christians often get it wrong, but tens of millions of quiet Christians daily seek, without fanfare or accolades, to get it right.

Jesus told his disciples they were to be light for the world, a city upon a hill that could not be hidden. They were to let their light shine by pursuing acts of kindness, mercy, and love. In this way Christ's followers were to incarnate—to embody and make visible—the love of God for humankind. In doing this they would become the evidence of God to the world. Christians are not meant to repel people from God, but by their very lives to draw people to God.

And that leads me to one final story. I was driving to church on Martin Luther King Jr. weekend, listening to an interview on NPR with the Reverend Billy Kyles. Billy was with Dr. King as he stood on the balcony of the Lorraine Motel in Memphis the morning he was killed. The interviewer asked what Rev. Kyles was preaching on that morning. He told the story of Robert Louis Stevenson who, as a boy, was sitting by his window looking intently outside. These were the days of gas streetlights and there, at the street, was the town lamplighter. He was carefully putting his ladder up against the lamppost, climbing up the ladder, and lighting the lantern. He would take it down, move down the street, and light the next one. Stevenson was asked, "What are you looking at so intently?" To which he replied, "I'm watching that man out there knock holes in the darkness."

This is what Jesus called his followers to do. It is what the church is meant to be about. By our acts of kindness and love we are called to knock holes in the darkness. I think young adults need to see Christians get it right. They need to see

Christians knocking holes in the darkness. When they do, there's little doubt that they will be interested once again in the gospel that inspires such actions.

If you've been turned off by Christians you've known, I'd invite you, as I did John, to get to know the real Jesus by reading one of the earliest accounts of his life and teachings. Read the Gospel According to Luke. It was as I read that Gospel as a teenager that I decided to follow this remarkable man. There are churches out there who seek to get it right. They are not perfect, but you would find in them a community of people who will welcome you, who will help you to know more about Jesus, and who will invite you to join them in knocking holes in the darkness.

God and
Public Schools

One reaction to the tragedy at Sandy Hook Elementary School in December 2012 has been a call to "put God back in the schools." I even heard one person suggest that the violence that happened in the school was because "we took God out of public schools." As a pastor I have a deep desire to lead people to God and encourage people to pray, read the Bible, and carry their faith into every part of their lives. But I've got a few questions about "putting God back in the schools."

In America our public schools are intended to be religiously neutral. Our teachers and schools are neither to endorse nor to inhibit religion. I believe this is a very good thing. When my kids were growing up I wanted their teachers to teach them science, reading, math, and history. I also wanted them to care about my kids. But I did not want my children's public school teachers teaching them religion. That was my job as a parent, and the job of our church, Sunday school, and youth group.

If we're going to put God back in schools, which God are we talking about? Within the Christian family alone there are often dramatically different ways of talking about God, whether by fundamentalists, evangelicals, Pentecostals, charismatics, moderates, progressives, liberals, Calvinists and Arminians, high-church and low-church—and these are just the Protestants! Add in Roman Catholics, Eastern Orthodox, and a host of groups that are often said to be outside the mainstream, and you begin to see the dilemma.

And while 78 percent of all Americans claim to be Christian, 22 percent claim another faith or no faith. If these numbers are applied to teachers, this would mean that one in five teachers may be Hindu or Muslim, Jewish or Buddhist, atheist or agnostic. Few of the folks calling for "putting God back in the schools" seem to be okay with people outside of the Christian faith teaching their children about God.

The religious neutrality in our schools is, I would argue, one of our strengths. Teachers cannot inhibit or deride religion. But this does not mean that we've taken God out of public schools. I'm reminded of the Book of Esther in the Bible. God is not explicitly mentioned in the book, but that did not mean that God was not at work in the story.

Christians believe that God is everywhere and is involved in our lives at every moment, whether we publicly acknowledge God or not. Most of the teachers I've met in public schools are people of faith. For many, their faith shapes how they approach their work as teachers. It strengthens, informs, and inspires them to love their students and to pursue their work with excellence. As in the book of Esther, they may not explicitly mention God, but God works through them nonetheless.

Students also bring their faith into the schools. They are free to pray any time, provided they are not disruptive. They are free to talk about their faith, provided they are not belligerent or hurtful to other students.

Getting It Right

Across the county, there are many churches and other religious groups who partner with public schools, not to evangelize but to provide real help. In the Kansas City area, the church I serve has partnered with six elementary schools in which a majority of the students live near the poverty line. We build playgrounds for these schools and paint and repair their buildings. We fund literacy efforts and provide free books. We ensure that each child has a winter coat, gloves, and hat, as well as school supplies, and we provide funds for special programs the schools otherwise could not afford. We also have tutoring programs with hundreds of volunteers who read to children and otherwise help the teachers and support their work. Every Friday we send backpacks with nutritious snacks home with 1,400 children who are at risk of being hungry on the weekends. We also distribute beds for children who we discover are sleeping on the floor in their homes. Our people are motivated by their faith to do these things. They don't talk about their faith, but it can clearly be seen in their actions.

I'm convinced many of America's heroes are public school teachers and administrators. Many of these people do what they do because of their faith. We don't need mandatory, non-sectarian prayers read over the loudspeaker to "put God back in the schools." God never left the schools. God is still at work through the hundreds of thousands of gifted teachers and administrators, committed parents, and passionate volunteers who seek to help give our children "a future with hope."

POSTSCRIPT

You may be wondering what happened with John. After our initial conversation, I asked John if he would come back and allow me to interview him before a camera so that I could share his perspectives both with my own congregation and with a broader audience of church leaders. Later that year he attended worship with us—it was the first time he'd been in church in years. Sometime later he asked if I would officiate at his wedding. I was honored that he asked, and I had the joy of sitting down with John and Nancy in preparation for their wedding. I enjoyed celebrating their union. One recent Christmas eve, I saw John, Nancy, and their little one in worship at our church. Several months later, in preparing this book, I asked John to read it and give me his feedback.

Has John become a Christian? No, not yet. I sense an openness I did not see the first time we met. And though we don't get the chance to talk often, I believe he values our relationship as do I. My hope and prayer is that one day he will become a follower of Jesus Christ.

This book is dedicated to him.

SEEING GRAY IN A WORLD
OF BLACK AND WHITE

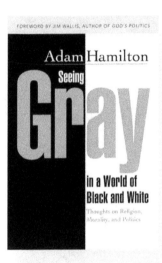

"Adam Hamilton is a thoughtful man whose writings will stretch your mind and heart."

—BILL HYBELS, Senior Pastor, Willow Creek Community Church and Chairman of the Board, Willow Creek Association

"When you list the best-known names in American Christianity—Billy Graham, Bill Hybels, Rick Warren, Max Lucado, Jim Wallis, and others—you probably don't yet think of Adam Hamilton. But you should, and I believe you will in the future."

—BRIAN MCLAREN, Author/Activist, brianmclaren.net

"We desperately need voices that can teach us to combine passionate conviction with charitable civility and honest self-examination. Adam Hamilton is one of those thoughtful voices, and *Seeing Gray* will help that conversation."

—JOHN ORTBERG, Author of *When the Game Is Over It All Goes Back In the Box*

ISBN: 978-1-4267-6662-6

WHY? MAKING SENSE OF GOD'S WILL

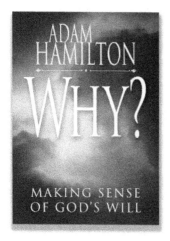

When the ground shakes, and a poor nation's economy is destroyed; when the waters rise, washing away a community's hopes and dreams; when a child suffers neglect and abuse; when violence tears apart nations; where is God?

In *Why? Making Sense of God's Will* best-selling author Adam Hamilton brings fresh insight to the age-old question of how to understand the will of God. Rejecting simplistic answers and unexamined assumptions, Hamilton addresses how we can comprehend God's plan for the world and ourselves.

"I recommend this book to anyone who longs to leave behind simplistic answers and discover a God who invites them into a collaborative process of bringing redemption, love and hope to a world in desperate need."

—**LYNNE HYBELS,**
   author of *Nice Girls Don't Change the World*

ISBN: 978-1-426-71478-8

d|Abingdon Press

AVAILABLE WHEREVER FINE BOOKS ARE SOLD.
For more information about Adam Hamilton, visit www.AdamHamilton.org

THE WAY: WALKING IN THE FOOTSTEPS OF JESUS

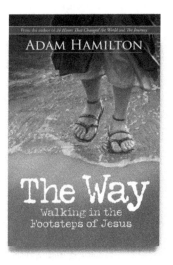

Adam Hamilton has visited the Holy Land to explore the birth of Jesus in *The Journey* and his death and resurrection in *24 Hours*. Now, join him as he follows in the footsteps of Jesus from the baptism and temptations and moving through his ministry: the people he loved, the healing he brought, the parables he taught and the enemies he made.

ISBN: 978-1-4267-5251-3

Also Available: 40 Day Devotional, DVD, Leader's guide, Children & Youth resources

Abingdon Press

AVAILABLE WHEREVER FINE BOOKS ARE SOLD.
For more information about Adam Hamilton, visit www.AdamHamilton.org

24 Hours That Changed the World

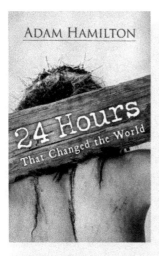

Walk with Jesus on his final day.
Sit beside him at the Last Supper.
Pray with him in Gethsemane.
Follow him to the cross.
Desert him. Deny him.
Experience the Resurrection.

No single event in human history has received more attention than the suffering and crucifixion of Jesus of Nazareth. In this heartbreaking, inspiring book, Adam Hamilton guides us, step by step, through the last 24 hours of Jesus' life.

"Adam Hamilton combines biblical story, historical detail, theological analysis, spiritual insight, and pastoral warmth to retell the narrative of Jesus' last and greatest hours."

—LEITH ANDERSON,

author of *The Jesus Revolution*

ISBN: 978-0-687-46555-2

Abingdon Press

Printed in the USA
CPSIA information can be obtained
at www.ICGtesting.com
JSHW070236190124
55486JS00008B/41

9 781426 775239